THE PSYCHOLOGIST'S BOOK
OF SELF-TESTS

THE PSYCHOLOGIST'S BOOK OF

SELF✓TESTS

25 Love, Sex, Intelligence, Career, and Personality Tests Developed by Professionals to Reveal the Real You

Louis Janda, Ph.D.

A PERIGEE BOOK

A Perigee Book
Published by The Berkley Publishing Group
200 Madison Avenue
New York, NY 10016

Copyright © 1996 by Dr. Louis Janda

Book design by Irving Perkins Associates

Cover design by Wendy Bass

First edition: July 1996

Published simultaneously in Canada.

The Putnam Berkley World Wide Web site address is
http://www.berkley.com

Library of Congress Cataloging-in-Publication Data
Janda, Louis H.
    The psychologist's book of self-tests : 25 love, sex,
    intelligence, career and personality tests developed by
    professionals to reveal the real you / Louis Janda. — 1st ed.
        p.   cm.
    ISBN 0-399-52211-5
    1. Personality tests.   2. Intelligence tests.   3. Love—Testing.
    4. Sex (Psychology)—Testing.   5. Work—Psychological aspects—
    Testing.   I. Title.
    BF698.5.J37   1996
    150'.28'7—dc20   95-49269
                                                                CIP

Printed in the United States of America

20 19 18 17 16 15 14 13

To my son, Christopher,
whom I love dearly, and who
has been testing me for the last twenty years

CONTENTS

SECTION III

GETTING ALONG

SECTION IV

GETTING TOGETHER

SECTION V

GETTING IT ON

Introduction

How many adjectives would you need to fully describe yourself? If you are like most people, you could probably come up with a half dozen without too much trouble. If pressed about other areas of your life, you might be able to add another half dozen, perhaps a dozen if you are especially introspective. And knowing about fifteen to twenty personal traits should be enough to provide a complete description for anyone. Right?

The answer is a resounding no if you rely upon the collective wisdom of the psychologists who have tackled this issue over the past century. Actually we psychologists haven't even come close to arriving at a consensus as to how many personal characteristics we need to have information about in order to describe a particular individual completely, but we have been extremely busy developing psychological tests to measure most any trait you might ever think of—and quite a few that you have probably never heard of. I can't give you anything more than an educated guess as to how many mental tests have been developed, but the figure is probably in the vicinity of 7000. One reference source published in 1983 describes more than 3500 tests.[1] Another that describes unpublished tests and personality scales contains information about nearly 2500 tests as of 1985. It seems reasonable to estimate that another 1000 tests have been added to these two lists over

---

[1]Psychologists use the terms "test," "scale," "instrument," "survey," and "schedule" interchangeably.

1

the past decade. And don't forget, many of these tests measure as many as a dozen traits at a time.

This does not mean, of course, that you would have to take 6000 tests to be able to have a complete picture of your mental functioning. The degree of overlap is almost mind-boggling. There are probably more than a hundred intelligence tests alone and well over a hundred tests of anxiety. Also, many of these tests measure arcane and trivial qualities that could only interest other psychologists. Do you really need to know, for instance, what your standardized score is with respect to your attitude toward female college professors?

While some existing tests seem so pointless that you have to wonder why anyone spent time developing them, a majority do deal with serious issues, and the intent has been either to help people improve their lot in life or to learn more about how we function as human beings. The myriad available aptitude tests, for instance, can help match one's abilities with a course of study or career direction. Clinical tests are routinely used by therapists to determine the best treatment for a patient. Personality researchers have developed tests that make us think about our behavior in everyday situations and consequently give us the option of modifying our responses so that we may have more satisfying and happier lives. Tests are not always used in the most appropriate way, but I truly believe they are one of the most important, if not the single most important, contribution psychologists have made to society. Tests really do have the potential to make our lives better and to make society fairer. My hope in putting together this book was to make these potential benefits available to a wider audience than usually has access to psychological testing. After you finish going through the tests included here, I will be gratified if you feel you have learned something important about yourself. I also hope you will have enjoyed the process. Self-discovery can be fun.

A Few Words About the Tests Used in This Book

There are two basic reasons why psychologists make the effort to develop a psychological test. First, they believe there is a need that remains to be filled on the part of clinicians, business, education, or any of the other institutions that use tests. Perhaps it is a need that has not been addressed previously, and the new test will be the first of its kind. Or the need may have been addressed by an existing test, but not as well as it might be. A new, improved version might be called for. If psychologists are successful in their efforts, their new tests are copyrighted and sold to those who find them useful. It would be unethical for me to reprint such tests here, even if I did obtain permission from the publisher. You might be asked to take one of these tests one day when you apply for a job or seek counseling for a personal problem, and it would bias the results if you had previous knowledge of the test.

But many of the tests that are developed with this goal in mind are never copyrighted. That does not necessarily mean that they were not the result of good work. The authors of tests face the same perils that all other creative people do. Perhaps the publisher did not see a large enough market for the new test. Perhaps it was viewed as being too similar to an existing test. Or, while it may have presented an improvement over an existing test, it was not seen as offering enough of a difference to compete successfully with older, established tests. The point is that there are many excellent tests that have never made it to market and are languishing in the scientific literature or a psychologist's file cabinet. Some of the tests you will find here come from this category.

The second major reason for developing tests is to help in conducting research on human abilities and personality. Suppose a researcher wants to learn more about self-esteem. The first step is to measure this characteristic in the men and women who will serve as subjects. And to measure it, you have to have a test. Later on, another researcher may have a slightly different theory about self-esteem, so a slightly different test must be developed. The result of this process is that there are dozens of tests of self-esteem available in the psychological literature, each measuring this personality variable from a slightly different angle, while all manage to capture the essence of this construct. The desire to learn more about human behavior has inspired the development of literally thousands of psychological tests.

Many of these tests are used a few times and quickly forgotten, but many others may be used in hundreds of research studies. This can mean that we may have better information about a test that was never for publication and sale than we do about some tests that are routinely used commercially. There are many fine tests that the public never sees unless someone takes an introductory psychology class and participates in an experiment as part of the course requirements. A majority of the tests used in this book come from this category.

All of the tests used here are true psychological tests. This means that established principles of test construction were used in their development, and information is available to give you a reasonable idea as to how you compare to others. Many of the tests you see in popular magazines are not really tests at all—at least not in the technical sense of the term. They are merely a collection of questions prepared by someone who may or may not have expertise in the area. And usually the guidelines you are given for interpreting your scores are nothing more than a reflection of the opinion of the preparer as to "what should be" rather than "what really is." The guidelines for interpreting your scores provided here are based on the responses, in almost all cases, of hundreds of men and women. When you finish taking one of these tests, you will have a good idea of how you compare to other people, because the guidelines are based on empirical results. They reflect more than my opinion or the opinion of the authors of a particular test.

How to Use This Book

I've included twenty-five tests in this book, grouped into five sections. The first section, called *Getting Ahead,* includes tests that are related to achieving success in your academic or career pursuits. The second section, *Getting It Together,* consists of tests that are especially relevant to psychological adjustment and mental health. Section three, *Getting Along,* will provide you with information that may be useful in improving your relationships with acquaintances and friends. *Getting Together,* the fourth section, provides you with tests that tap various aspects of your romantic relationships. For this section and the next, you might want to have your partner take the tests as well so you can compare your answers. You might just learn something about your compatibility. The last section, *Getting It On,* deals with your sexuality. There is no need to follow my order. You can examine the sections according to your own interests and needs. Nor do you have to take the tests in any section in the order in which I've presented them. Some tests are more closely interrelated than others, but essentially they all stand alone.

Two criteria that I had in mind when I selected a test were that it deal with an important human characteristic and that it be interesting to take and to think about once you have the results. For those tests that measure characteristics that may be interfering with your ability to have a satisfying life, I have added a few thoughts as to how you can go about changing. I hope that you will have learned something about psychology and human behavior as well as something about yourself by the time you finish with this book.

A Few Words About Norms

Now for a very brief statistics lesson. Psychologists who develop true psychological tests collect information about the responses of large numbers of men and women so that subsequent test-takers can have a basis for seeing how they stand relative to others. This original group of men and women, called a standardization sample, provides the information that are used in developing norms. So norms are nothing more than a summary of the scores of a large group of men and women that allows you to make a comparison—a comparison between your score and that of the standardization sample.

There are a variety of ways in which norms can be expressed, and I have selected the simplest and most straightforward for you to use—percentiles. I'm sure you all remember percentiles from all those achievement tests you took in school, but let me refresh your memory anyway. A percentile score tells you how you compare to the standardization sample and, by inference, to the rest of society. So if you have a percentile score of 15, that means that your score is equal to or higher than the scores of 15 percent of the people who take the test. The higher your percentile score, the higher you rank on that test compared to others who have taken it.

I've used five reference points for you to use when interpreting your scores—percentiles of 15, 30, 50, 70, and 85. This will allow you to determine if your score is average, modestly above or below average, or substantially above or below average. This should provide you with sufficient information to allow you to obtain a sense of your strengths and weaknesses.

As I mentioned above, many of the tests used in this book were developed by research psychologists to learn more about human personality. Since these psychologists usually work at universities, they use the subjects available to them, namely college students. So, many of the norms used here are based on the responses of young adults. If you are considerably older than the typical college student, it may have an effect on the interpretation of your score. I'll remind you of this when it seems especially relevant to what your test score might mean.

A Cautionary Note

Bear with me just a moment longer before you begin. All of the tests included in this book were developed with a normal population in mind. They were not designed to detect extreme cases or severe pathology. You may be pleased by the results of some of your tests, and you may be distressed by the results of others. But in either case, the results do not mean that you are a candidate for sainthood, nor do they mean you should be checking into the nearest psychiatric hospital. Please use the information from each test as it was intended—as a vehicle to learn more about yourself and how you compare with other people. This book is not intended to provide a substitute for a professional evaluation, and you should not think of it as such. It can provide you with a sense of your strengths, and it can provide you with some direction in your quest for self-improvement.

OK. Time to get started. Be honest with yourself, keep an open mind, and most of all, have fun!

GETTING AHEAD

This section measures skills and characteristics you need to be successful in college or your career. After you complete the tests in this section, you will know—

   A. How intelligent you are.
   B. How much you fear success.
   C. How skillful you are in finding the right job.
   D. How comfortable you are with your success.
   E. How smart you are about taking tests.

How Intelligent Are You?

✓

THE GENERAL MENTAL
ABILITIES TEST

DIRECTIONS: The following test contains five sections, all of which consist of multiple-choice questions. You may take as long as you like to answer the questions.

ANALOGIES

For the following items, select the alternative that best completes the sentence.

_____ 1. Scant is to deficient as sedate is to _____.
   a. serene
   b. moody
   c. frivolous
   d. flippant

_____ 2. Renounce is to accept as imperfect is to _____.
   a. defective
   b. deficient
   c. flawless
   d. scanty

_____ 3. Lack is to surplus as renounce is to _____.
   a. abjure
   b. accept
   c. repudiate
   d. abdicate

_____ 4. Ascertain is to learn as petty is to _____.
    a. trivial
    b. magnanimous
    c. significant
    d. substantial

_____ 5. Essential is to fundamental as endorse is to _____.
    a. sanction
    b. condemn
    c. denounce
    d. reprove

_____ 6. Exile is to ostracize as ethical is to _____.
    a. immoral
    b. honorable
    c. promiscuous
    d. lecherous

_____ 7. Oppression is to justice as obtain is to _____.
    a. forgo
    b. purchase
    c. procure
    d. acquire

_____ 8. Sheer is to opaque as parallel is to _____.
    a. analogous
    b. coinciding
    c. divergent
    d. similar

_____ 9. Remit is to retain as nasty is to _____.
    a. repellent
    b. odious
    c. beastly
    d. delightful

_____10. Bat is to human as whale is to _____.
   a. frog
   b. bear
   c. bird
   d. carp

_____11. Efface is to obliterate as general is to _____.
   a. inexact
   b. exact
   c. extinct
   d. specific

_____12. Large is to minute as pacific is to _____.
   a. bellicose
   b. halcyon
   c. tranquil
   d. placid

VOCABULARY

Each word in capital letters is followed by four words. Pick the word that comes closest in meaning to the word in capitals.

_____13. CABINET
   a. bureau
   b. federal
   c. open
   d. drawer

_____14. OBSTACLE
   a. impediment
   b. gate
   c. yard
   d. gateway

_____15. CONTENT
   a. shape
   b. hinder
   c. satisfied
   d. appalled

_____16. ABDICATE
   a. appease
   b. suggest
   c. dictate
   d. resign

_____17. LOQUACIOUS
   a. parsimonious
   b. courageous
   c. verbose
   d. cautious

_____18. LITURGY
   a. livid
   b. angry
   c. ritual
   d. spoiled

_____19. PASTORAL
   a. religious
   b. graze
   c. neglect
   d. peaceful

_____20. MOPE
   a. stupid
   b. relax
   c. clean
   d. apathetic

_____21. LACONIC
   a. concise
   b. intelligent
   c. colorful
   d. quiet

_____22. SERPENTINE
   a. treacherous
   b. frightening
   c. misleading
   d. silly

_____23. MISCREANT
   a. villain
   b. incorrect
   c. ineptitude
   d. fortuitous

_____24. OSTENTATIOUS
   a. generous
   b. brilliance
   c. pecuniary
   d. pretentious

GENERAL INFORMATION

For each of the following items, select the correct answer.

_____25. What is the first month of the year that has exactly 30 days?
   a. January
   b. February
   c. March
   d. April

_____26. What planet has the shortest year?
   a. Earth
   b. Pluto
   c. Mercury
   d. Uranus

_____27. What is the world's northernmost national capital?
   a. Stockholm
   b. London
   c. Reykjavik
   d. Oslo

_____28. To the nearest day, how long does it take the moon to revolve around the Earth?
   a. 1 day
   b. 27 days
   c. 30 days
   d. 365 days

_____29. What is the Fahrenheit equivalent of 0 degrees Celsius?
   a. –32 degrees
   b. 0 degrees
   c. 32 degrees
   d. 212 degrees

_____30. How many dimensions does a solid have?
   a. one
   b. two
   c. three
   d. four

_____31. Who wrote *Gone With the Wind?*
   a. Sylvia Plath
   b. Scarlett O'Hara
   c. Gertrude Stein
   d. Margaret Mitchell

_____32. In what month is Groundhog Day?
   a. January
   b. February
   c. March
   d. May

_____33. What is "The Windy City"?
   a. New York
   b. Detroit
   c. Chicago
   d. San Francisco

_____34. How many miles are there in a kilometer?
   a. .4
   b. .6
   c. 1
   d. 1.6

_____35. Who holds the record for career home runs?
   a. Babe Ruth
   b. Lou Gehrig
   c. Mickey Mantle
   d. Hank Aaron

_____36. What two cities were the subject of Dickens's *A Tale of Two Cities?*
   a. London and Madrid
   b. London and Paris
   c. London and Berlin
   d. London and New York

MATHEMATICAL ABILITY

For each of the following items, select the correct answer. You may use scratch paper.

_____37. If 2x + y = 5, then 6x + 3y = ?
   a. 2/5
   b. 3/9
   c. 15
   d. 18

_____38. One side of a rectangle is 3 feet long and the diagonal is 5 feet long. What is its area?
   a. 6
   b. 7.5
   c. 12
   d. 15

_____39. Rosanne's trail mix uses 6 ounces of M&Ms for every 9 ounces of Hershey's Kisses. How many ounces of M&Ms are needed for 75 ounces of trail mix?
   a. 25
   b. 30
   c. 32.5
   d. 36

_____40. The diagonal of a rectangle is 5 feet, and one side is 4 feet long. What is the perimeter?
   a. 12 feet
   b. 14 feet
   c. 16 feet
   d. 18 feet

_____41. A club of 60 people has 36 men. What percentage of the club is women?
    a. 20 percent
    b. 24 percent
    c. 40 percent
    d. 48 percent

_____42. The average of 3 single-digit numbers is 7. The smallest that one of the numbers can be is:
    a. 0
    b. 1
    c. 2
    d. 3

_____43. The hypotenuse of a right triangle is 5 feet long, and its area is 6 square feet. One of the sides of the triangle is:
    a. 1.2 feet
    b. 2 feet
    c. 2.5 feet
    d. 4 feet

_____44. $1/4 \times 2/3 \times 3/2 = ?$
    a. 1/4
    b. 5/9
    c. 6/9
    d. 3

_____45. $1/4 \times 3/4 \div 4/5 = ?$
    a. 7/13
    b. 15/64
    c. 15/4
    d. 12/20

_____ 46. Which of the following is the largest number?
   a. 13/24
   b. 21/40
   c. 36/70
   d. 51/100

_____ 47. Sally is 2 years older than her brother. Twelve years ago, she was twice as old as he was. How old is Sally now?
   a. 14
   b. 16
   c. 20
   d. 32

_____ 48. There were 16 teams in a basketball tournament. When a team lost, it was eliminated from the tournament. How many games had to be played to determine a champion?
   a. 4
   b. 9
   c. 15
   d. 31

SPATIAL ABILITY

For the following items, your task is to select the picture on the right that would result if the pieces on the left side of the page were put together properly. There is only one correct answer for each item.

49.

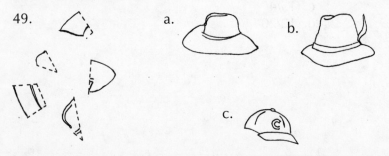

50.

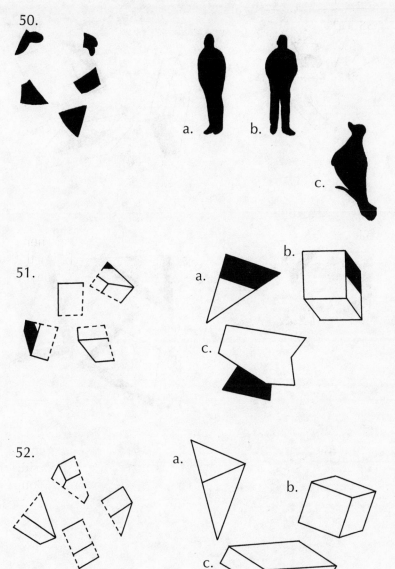

51.

52.

53.

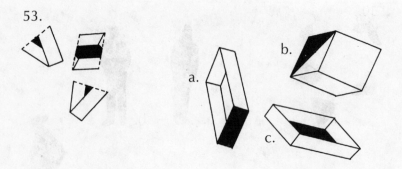

54.

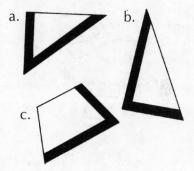

SOURCE: Louis H. Janda, Jerry Fulk, Meredith Janda, and Judy Wallace. "The Development of a Test of General Mental Abilities." Unpublished manuscript, 1995. Old Dominion University.

SCORING KEY

1. a	19. d	37. c
2. c	20. d	38. c
3. b	21. a	39. b
4. a	22. a	40. b
5. a	23. a	41. c
6. b	24. d	42. d
7. a	25. d	43. d
8. c	26. c	44. a
9. d	27. c	45. b
10. b	28. b	46. a
11. a	29. c	47. b
12. a	30. c	48. c
13. a	31. d	49. a
14. a	32. b	50. a
15. c	33. c	51. b
16. d	34. b	52. c
17. c	35. d	53. c
18. c	36. b	54. b

HOW DO YOU COMPARE?

Score	Percentile
18	15
22	30
27	50
32	70
36	85
45	Gifted

About Intelligence

The General Mental Abilities Test was constructed to measure intelligence. Although this test is not as comprehensive as most established tests of intelligence, it will give you a rough idea of where you stand with regard to your intellectual abilities. In our validation studies, we found that scores on the test did predict grade point averages of college undergraduates as well as their SAT scores. Because the norms for this test are based upon the performance of college students, a score at the 50th percentile means that you are somewhat above average in ability; that is, you have as much ability as the average college student. If you answered at least 45 of the items correct, the chances are good that you would score in the superior range of other established tests of intelligence.

So what does it mean if you obtained a high score on this test? Consider yourself fortunate. It is a clear advantage to be born intelligent. People with high IQ scores get better grades in school, score better on achievement tests, go further in school, and have a greater likelihood of having a professional career. Also, there is a tendency for extremely bright people to have higher self-esteem, more energy, more athletic ability, happier marriages, and even better sex lives. These people also have a lower than average incidence of a variety of problems, including severe psychological problems, alcoholism, and criminality. Of course there are exceptions, but taken as a whole, highly intelligent people do stand out in a number of ways.

You high scorers shouldn't be too smug, though. A high IQ score is by no means a guarantee of success. Every year countless college students with impressive College Board Scores flunk out of school while their modestly endowed peers make the Dean's list. And I still remember a talk I gave many years ago to a local chapter of MENSA—a club for which you are eligible only if you demonstrate that your intelligence places you in the top two percent of the population. (A score of 45 on this test would be at about this level). I can't think of a polite way to say it—they were one boring group of people. My theory was that because they hadn't done much with their lives, they joined the club to be able to prove to themselves what superior people they were. But the reality is that qualities such as motivation, perseverance, and curiosity more than make up for a modest IQ score. What you do with your life is much more important than how you score on a standardized test.

As evidence of the importance of personality characteristics, it has been demonstrated that while intelligence does predict one's level of occupational status, it does not predict one's degree of success within a particular occupational level. So if you are bright enough to make it through medical school, for example, you have as much of a chance to be a successful physician as your more intelligent classmates. It does require a certain level of intelligence to master complex material, but as long as you have the requisite mental ability, your personal qualities will then determine how good you are in your chosen field.

There is no doubt that there is a substantial genetic component to intelligence (only a handful of politically correct psychologists deny this well-established fact of life). We all know that bright parents tend to have bright children. But this does not mean that intelligence is immutable. One's experiences can, and do, influence one's intellectual functioning. A strong curiosity and desire to learn can cause intelligence to increase—and this process can continue throughout one's life span.

There are, however, limits to how much IQ can be increased. Forrest Gump would never win the Nobel Prize for physics no matter how much stimulation he received.

But if you had trouble keeping up with your classmates in school, you might surpass many of them as an adult if you are determined to do so.

Another important aspect of intelligence is that it is not evenly distributed within an individual. To some extent, an IQ score reflects an average of many different abilities. For example, I always did well in any course involving numbers, but I could never understand how my English instructors could get so much out of a Joseph Conrad novel (actually, I still think they made up a lot of that stuff). And while I'm tough to beat in Trivial Pursuit, I've never won a game of Scrabble in my life. So even if you were discouraged about your score on this test, it does not mean that you could not be exceptional in some way. James Watson, who won the Nobel Prize for unraveling the structure of DNA, has written that he scored only slightly above average on an IQ test.

The primary advantage of intelligence is that it does make a lot of things a little bit easier. It is easier to get through school, it is easier to pass the professional licensure exam, and it is easier to adapt when your boss decides to change the software everyone must use.

But having above average intelligence can have a downside. Some of the most successful people I know had to struggle to get where they are. My wife has a friend who had to take the exam for licensure as a real estate agent three times before passing it. And she studied hard for each test. But once she passed, her career took off like a rocket. She was used to working hard to compensate for the fact that things did not come easily for her and her habits guaranteed her success.

So for those of you who did have high scores on this test—don't be complacent. You may not find it difficult to get into that prestigious school or pass the test for a promotion, but unless you are willing to work hard, you may find yourself stagnating. And for those of you who had below average scores—don't despair. Discover what your particular strength is, and then let your determination and hard work take you where you want to go.

Are You Afraid to Succeed?

THE FEAR OF SUCCESS SCALE

DIRECTIONS: For the following items, if the statement is mostly true of you, respond with a T. If it is mostly false, respond with an F.

_____ 1. I am sometimes afraid to do things as well as I know I could.

_____ 2. I am prone to worry that I may antagonize others if my work is of superior quality.

_____ 3. I never worry about the possibility of being disliked by others for doing well at something.

_____ 4. I sometimes do less than my very best so that no one will be threatened.

_____ 5. I often worry about the possibility that others will think I am a "show-off."

_____ 6. I never worry about the possibility that others may think I work too hard.

_____ 7. I would find it nerve-wracking to be regarded as one of the best in my field.

_____ 8. I seem to be more anxious after succeeding at something than after failing at something.

_____ 9. I would worry that others might think I was peculiar or strange if I were too devoted to my work.

_____ 10. I have occasionally deliberately done average or mediocre work in order to make sure that someone else would do better than I.

_____ 11. I sometimes worry that others will expect too much of me.

_____ 12. I usually set goals for myself that are lower than what I am capable of reaching.

_____ 13. I seem to be drawn to activities that are not very challenging.

_____ 14. I do not seem to enjoy doing superior work as much as I feel that I should.

_____ 15. I do not like competing with others if there is a possibility that hard feelings toward me may develop.

_____ 16. I worry about the possibility of being criticized by my friends or associates for being too involved with my own work.

_____ 17. I sometimes worry that I may become too well informed for my own good.

_____ 18. I never worry about the possibility that friendships may have to be sacrificed in order to accomplish certain tasks or kinds of work.

_____ 19. If I were outstanding at something, I would worry about the possibility of others making fun of me behind my back.

_____20. I do not worry about the personal feelings of others when it comes to getting something important done.

_____21. I have a tendency to worry that someone may become jealous if I do well at something.

_____22. I would never worry about the possibility that academic or occupational success might interfere with success in social relationships.

_____23. I would never worry about the possibility that others might feel uncomfortable or ill at ease around me if I were too competent at something.

_____24. I have a tendency to fear that others might like me only for what I could do for them due to my competency in a certain field.

_____25. I am prone to worry that undue pressures would be placed on me if I were to develop considerable competency in some field.

_____26. I worry that I may become so knowledgeable that others will not like me.

_____27. I would worry that others might try to take advantage of me if I were extremely competent at something.

_____28. If I were to do well at something, I would worry that someone might try to undermine my success.

_____29. I would worry that others might be afraid of me if they felt that I understood people too well.

SOURCE: Lawrence R. Good and Katherine C. Good. "An objective measure of the motive to avoid success." *Psychological Reports*, 1973, *33*, 1009–1010. Used by permission.

SCORING KEY

1. T	11. T	21. T
2. T	12. T	22. F
3. F	13. T	23. F
4. T	14. T	24. T
5. T	15. T	25. T
6. F	16. T	26. T
7. T	17. T	27. T
8. T	18. F	28. T
9. T	19. T	29. T
10. T	20. F	

HOW DO YOU COMPARE?

SCORES		PERCENTILES
Men	Women	
2	3	15
4	5	30
6	8	50
8	11	70
10	13	85

About Fear of Success

In the late 1960s, psychologist Martina Horner generated widespread interest in the concept of "Fear of Success" when she reported that women were much more likely to exhibit this tendency than were men. In her research, Horner asked college women to write a paragraph in response to the lead sentence, "After first term finals, Ann finds herself at the top of her medical school class . . ." College men were given the same sentence, only the name

John was substituted for Ann. The results were dramatic. Fully 62 percent of the women wrote paragraphs detailing a variety of unpleasant consequences of Ann's success. As an example, one woman wrote, "Ann is an acne-faced book-worm. She runs to the bulletin board and finds she's on top. As usual, she smarts off. A chorus of groans is the rest of the class's reply." In contrast, only 9 percent of the men suggested that there was anything negative about "John's" success. John was typically described as a conscientious, hardworking, likable guy. Horner's work inspired a flurry of research activity (the Fear of Success Scale presented here is one example) as well as numerous articles in popular magazines. It didn't take long before many women were convinced that they had yet one more obstacle to overcome.

Although subsequent research did not receive nearly as much attention, it did suggest that women may not be as crippled by their fears as Horner's work suggested. First, several studies (including one by yours truly) found that fear of success seems to be related to the degree to which a vocation is seen as being dominated by men or women. For example, women will express more fear of success when Ann is at the top of her engineering class, but men express more fear of success when John succeeds in nursing school. Both men and women may experience feelings of discomfort about succeeding in a field that is dominated by the other sex. Second, the subsequent research raised questions about the way in which Horner measured fear of success. When other researchers used more sophisticated methods, the differences between men and women were greatly reduced and in some cases disappeared.

Even if women do not experience as much fear of success as Horner claimed, they probably do have legitimate reasons for being concerned about standing out in some situations. Many high school girls, and even college women, have reported that they try not to let their high grades become generally known because they believe that it might impair their chances of being asked for a date. Men may say they prefer intelligent women, but it is an unusual man who feels comfortable with a woman he knows is smarter or more capable than he is. As a second example, a friend of mine who recently graduated from medical school is convinced the faculty gave her a more difficult time than the men in her class. Medical school faculties continue to be dominated by men even in this day and age, when close to half of the students are women, and at least some faculty members seem to resent the changing gender composition of their profession. The women in my friend's class, especially the most capable and brightest, were regularly belittled and humiliated. In such a situation, most anyone might find it easier to blend in with the crowd than to stand out as a result of their accomplishments.

Fear of success is a real problem for some people, but I believe a more common, and possibly related problem is fear of failure. Both fear of success and fear of failure can have similar effects—they prevent people from making their best effort. If a student makes less than his best effort on a term paper, then he can reassure himself that he didn't really try when he receives a C. When an athlete slacks off in training, then she can rationalize that her opponent was in better shape—but not more skillful—when she loses the match.

It can be nearly impossible to distinguish between fear of success and fear of failure because their effects can be so similar. I have a friend named Tom who is a very talented painter, but he has never entered his work in any of the local art shows. A few years ago I received one of his paintings as a gift, and when I took it to an art store to be framed, the owner asked me to have Tom get in touch with him. Based on seeing one example of Tom's work, he believed he could sell Tom's other paintings. Tom declined to get in touch with the owner even though he was desperate for money. Was his reluctance fear of success or fear of failure? I don't know, but to borrow a line from Ed of the television show *Northern Exposure,* when opportunity came knocking, Tom tiptoed out the back door.

If you did receive a score at the 85th percentile or higher, you may benefit from taking a close look at yourself. If you are young, say in your mid-20s, the chances are you will grow more comfortable with success as you gain more experience. It is not uncommon for people who are in school or just beginning their careers to feel uncomfortable with the recognition that comes with success. They may feel they don't deserve it. But as time goes on, most people come to realize they do deserve the recognition every bit as much as their colleagues.

If age and experience has not helped you feel comfortable with the idea of success, you should make a conscious effort to deal with this self-defeating tendency. You might make a list of the situations in which your fears are holding you back. Then make a list of the negative consequences of success that concern you. Often simply having a clear conceptualization of the problem will help you get past it. If need be, though, try making a deliberate effort to confront every situation on your first list and then record how many events on your second list actually occur.

Fear of success is almost always a subtle problem. There are a few people, and my friend Tom may be one of them, whose lives are greatly affected by their fears. But for most of us, fear of success may simply be one of those things that causes us some discomfort as we're beginning to spread our wings.

How Good Are Your
Job-Hunting Skills?

THE ASSERTIVE JOB-HUNTING
SURVEY

DIRECTIONS: This inventory is designed to provide information about the way in which you look for a job. Picture yourself in each of these job-hunting situations and indicate how likely it is you would respond in the described manner. If you have never job-hunted before, answer according to how you would like to try to find a job. Please respond to the following statements by using a number from the key below.

> 1 = Very unlikely
> 2 = Unlikely
> 3 = Somewhat unlikely
> 4 = Somewhat likely
> 5 = Likely
> 6 = Very likely

_____ 1. When asked to indicate my experience for a position, I would mention only my paid work experience.

_____ 2. If I heard someone talking about an interesting job opening, I'd be reluctant to ask for more information unless I knew the person.

_____ 3. I would ask an employer who did not have an opening if he knew of other employers who might have job openings.

_____ 4. I would downplay my qualifications so that an employer won't think I'm more qualified than I am.

_____ 5. I would rather use an employment agency to find a job than apply to employers directly.

_____ 6. Before an interview, I would contact an employee of the organization to learn more about that organization.

_____ 7. I would hesitate to ask questions when I was being interviewed for a job.

_____ 8. I would avoid contacting potential employers by phone or in person because I would feel they are too busy to talk with me.

_____ 9. If an interviewer were very late for my interview, I would leave or arrange for another appointment.

_____ 10. I believe an experienced employment counselor would have a better idea of what jobs I should apply for than I would have.

_____ 11. If a secretary told me that a potential employer was too busy to see me, I would stop trying to contact that employer.

_____ 12. Getting the job I want is largely a matter of luck.

_____13. I'd directly contact the person for whom I would be working, rather than the personnel department of an organization.

_____14. I would be reluctant to ask professors or supervisors to write letters of recommendation for me.

_____15. I would not apply for a job unless I had all the qualifications listed on the published job description.

_____16. I would ask an employer for a second interview if I felt the first one went poorly.

_____17. I would be reluctant to contact an organization about employment unless I know there is a job opening.

_____18. If I didn't get a job I would call the employer and ask how I could improve my chances for a similar position.

_____19. I would feel uncomfortable asking friends for job leads.

_____20. With the job market as tight as it is, I had better take whatever job I can get.

_____21. If the personnel office refused to refer me for an interview, I would directly contact the person I wanted to work for if I felt qualified for the position.

_____22. I would rather interview with recruiters who come to the college campus or job fairs than contact employers directly.

_____23. If an interviewer says, "I'll contact you if there are any openings," I would figure there's nothing else I can do.

_____24. I'd check out available job openings before deciding what kind of job I'd like to have.

_____25. I would be reluctant to contact someone I don't know for information about career fields in which I am interested.

SOURCE: Heather A. Becker. "The Assertive Job-Hunting Survey." *Measurement and Evaluation in Guidance*, 1980, *13*, 43–48. Used by permission.

SCORING KEY

Add your points for the following items: 3, 6, 9, 13, 16, 18, and 21.

The remaining items are "reverse scored." To obtain your points for these items, subtract the number you indicated from 7. Add the subsequent numbers together and find your total score by adding the totals for the two clusters of items. The reverse scored items are: 1, 2, 4, 5, 7, 8, 10, 11, 12, 14, 15, 17, 19, 20, 22, 23, 24, and 25.

HOW DO YOU COMPARE?

SCORE	PERCENTILE
90	15
98	30
106	50
116	70
124	85

About Job-Hunting Assertiveness

The author of the Assertive Job-Hunting Survey, Dr. Heather Becker, designed it to be used at the Career Counseling Center at the University of Texas where she works. One of Dr. Becker's tasks was to conduct workshops for students, mostly seniors about to graduate, who wanted to increase the odds of having their job-hunting experiences end in success. Along with other members of the Center, Dr. Becker wrote the items to reflect the topics discussed and the skills taught at the workshop.

Everyone has heard the statistic that 80 percent of job openings are not advertised, and if you look at the classified ads in any large newspaper, it is easy to believe this. Except for fields where there is an undersupply of qualified applicants, such as the computer field, a substantial majority of ads are for entry-level jobs or for sales positions. Passive, nonassertive men and women who wait for an invitation to apply for a job will either be left out in the cold or end up in positions that they may not be happy with.

In using this scale in her workshops, Becker found that some strategies were especially difficult for students to utilize. Let us take a closer look at a few of the items that reflect these skills and that a majority of students reported they were unlikely to do. The first of these is item 6, which suggests that before one's interview it is a good idea to contact an employee to learn more about the company. Employers want enthusiastic, knowledgeable employees, so obviously the more you know about the company, the more you are likely to impress your potential employer. It may seem awkward to call someone you don't know and ask questions about his or her job, but the information you get could be invaluable. R. N. Bolles, author of the best-selling book, *What Color Is Your Parachute? A Practical Manual for Job-Hunters and Career-Changers,* has suggested

that applicants should identify a specific problem that the
company has and develop a strategy for solving it before
the first interview. You may be able to learn a lot about a
company from annual reports and business journals, but
what better way to learn about its problems than by talking with an employee? And besides, most people love talking about their problems at work.

The second item that reflected a pervasive lack of assertiveness was number 10, which suggests that an experienced employment counselor would have a better idea of
what type of jobs you're qualified for than you do. Employment counselors can be an excellent source of information, but they are not nearly as interested in your finding
the best possible job as you are. Nor will they ever know
your strengths and abilities as well as you do. If you have
access to employment counselors, use them to get ideas,
but don't ever let them tell you what jobs you are or are
not qualified for.

The next key item is number 13, which suggests that you
should contact the person you would be working for directly rather than applying to the personnel department.
The personnel department probably has a checklist of the
requisite qualifications for the position, and if you don't
match the list exactly, you're out of luck. If you can talk to
the person you would be working for, you might be able to
convince him or her that your background and skills are
just what is needed, even if you happen to be six months
short of the necessary experience. This would be especially
true if you've done your homework and learned what specific problems need solving.

The fourth item is number 22, which expresses a preference to talk to recruiters at college campuses or job fairs
rather than contacting employers directly. It certainly is easier to visit a job fair and talk to a recruiter who you know is
eager to talk to applicants, but that is the passive approach

and is less likely to result in success than contacting the employer directly. First of all, the same limitations that apply to the personnel office apply to recruiters. Second, the recruiter may talk with hundreds of applicants, so you are likely to be lost in the crowd. And third, employers are always looking for people with initiative, so the more assertive you can be—without being obnoxious, of course—the more likely you are to get the job.

The final item I want to discuss is number 24. Most people indicated that they would check out available job openings before deciding what kind of job they would like. I admit that it is certainly more practical to pursue a career in which there is an abundance of opportunity, but this strategy may backfire in the long run. Even if you love English literature, you may still have an easier time finding a job if you major in computer science, but the odds are you will be miserable before long. If you are serious and dedicated, you can eventually succeed in a field you love no matter how limited the opportunities may be. I could tell you several stories of people who earned Ph.D.s in fields such as history and English, in which it can be extremely difficult to find a faculty position. Some of these people drove cabs for a while, some taught part-time at community colleges for virtually no pay, but the ones who really cared eventually found a position that suited their background. These people had a few tough years, but not nearly as many as they would have had if they had gone into a field they didn't enjoy.

If your attempts to find the right job have been less than successful, use the items on Becker's scale as a guide for improving your job-hunting skills. If you scored four or lower on an item, endeavor to become more assertive in that regard. The meek may inherit the earth, but they don't get the best jobs.

How Comfortable Are You With Success?

> ✓
>
> ## THE IMPOSTOR PHENOMENON SCALE

DIRECTIONS: Below are statements indicating feelings and attitudes about yourself and your abilities. Please indicate how true you feel these statements are as they apply to you using the guidelines below:

NOT TRUE   1   2   3   4   5   6   7   VERY
   AT ALL   TRUE

_____ 1. In general, people tend to believe I am more competent than I am.

_____ 2. I am certain my present level of achievement results from true ability.

_____ 3. Sometimes I am afraid I will be discovered for who I really am.

_____ 4. I find it easy to accept compliments about my intelligence.

_____ 5. I feel I deserve whatever honors, recognition, or praise I receive.

_____ 6. At times I have felt I am in my present position or academic program through some kind of mistake.

_____ 7. I feel confident that I will succeed in the future.

_____ 8. I tend to feel like a phony.

_____ 9. My personality or charm often makes a strong impression on people in authority.

_____10. I consider my accomplishments adequate for this stage in my life.

_____11. In discussion, if I disagree with my professor or boss, I speak out.

_____12. I often achieve success on a project or test when I have anticipated I would fail.

_____13. I often feel I am concealing secrets about myself from others.

_____14. My public and private self are the same.

SOURCE: Pauline Rose Clance. "The Impostor Phenomenon Scale." *Psychotherapy: Theory, Research and Practice,* 1978, 241–247. Used by permission; not to be reproduced in any form without the written permission of Dr. Pauline Clance.

SCORING KEY FOR THE IMPOSTOR PHENOMENON SCALE

Add together your responses for items 1, 3, 6, 8, 12, and 13. The remaining items are reverse scored, so for items 2, 4, 5, 7, 9, 10, 11, and 14 perform the following transformation before adding your responses together: $1 = 7$; $2 = 6$; $3 = 5$; $4 = 4$; $5 = 3$; $6 = 2$; and $7 = 1$. For your total score, add the numbers for the two groups of items together.

HOW DO YOU COMPARE?

Score		Percentile
Men	*Women*	
17	18	15
22	24	30
27	29	50
32	34	70
37	40	85

About the Impostor Phenomenon

Boy, do I know about this one. When I first arrived on the campus of Arizona State University as a graduate student admitted into the Ph.D. program in clinical psychology, I was sure that I was just lucky. They probably had already filled their class and someone backed out at the last minute, so they invited me to join the program simply to make the first-year class a nice even number. I didn't belong there, I was convinced, and I would never make it through the first year.

It didn't take me too long to accept that I could compete with my classmates. I received the only perfect score on the first statistics exam, so I had to be at least as intelligent as everyone else.

But the feeling of being an impostor surfaced many more times throughout the years that followed. I had the same feeling when I first arrived at Old Dominion University as a brand-new assistant professor. It was pure luck that I was hired, and I didn't stand a chance of getting tenure. But before that first year was over I had three articles accepted for publication in prestigious journals, so I figured I belonged there after all.

This feeling of being out of my league came back even stronger the first time I went to New York to meet with an editor who had expressed an interest in publishing my first textbook. Only really important people wrote books, much less had their way paid to New York. What the hell was I doing there? She was sure to see right through me. But I was offered the contract, and the book was a success, so I knew it wasn't only "really important people" who published books—ordinary people like me did it too.

It's been a quarter of a century since I attended my first class as a graduate student, and nowadays it is rare that I feel like an impostor. But the feeling does continue to affect me in more subtle ways. When she gets really exasperated with me, my wife Meredith tells me that there is no pleasing me. When I have a book proposal, I worry that I'll never find an editor who wants to buy it. Then when I do sign a book contract and am busy writing, I worry that it is so bad that the editor will cancel the contract and it will never get published. I continue to have some trouble enjoying the modest success that I have had.

There are a couple of ways that one develops the feeling of being an impostor. The route that I took was being reared in a working-class family with parents who never entertained the thought of going to college. I never even knew anyone whose parents went to college until I was twelve. I remember my mother and father talking about how wonderful it would be if I could actually be a college graduate some day. That I might go beyond a bachelor's degree never occurred to them in their wildest imagination. Doctors, lawyers, and college professors might as well have come from a different planet. They sure didn't come from my neighborhood. So, in retrospect, it is not surprising that I felt I did not belong there when I arrived on the Arizona State University campus. No one in my family had ever done such a thing, and they had never imagined that I could either.

The second type of impostor is one whose parents complimented him or her lavishly, but for qualities other than the ones needed for success. I know a woman—I'll call her Susan—who is extremely bright and competent in her profession. As a child, Susan was told virtually every day by her parents how pretty and charming she was. She would be a big success one day, according to Mom and Dad, because no one would be able to resist her charms. Well, her parents were right. Susan is very successful. But she can't get past the nagging feeling that it's not her talent, but the fact that people like and admire her, that has led to her success.

Like me, Susan has been around long enough to know that she really does belong in her profession. She knows that her looks and charm alone could not have sustained a 20-year career. But she wonders if she had begun her career without such a strong sense of being an impostor, could she have accomplished even more? Would she have tackled even more difficult projects? Would she have applied for positions at more prestigious universities? Maybe she could have been a college president, had she only believed such a thing was possible.

If you had a high score on the impostor phenomenon scale, you probably already know how it can affect you. Like Susan and me, you may have difficulty in accepting and enjoying the successes you do experience, and you may set unnecessary limits on just how far you can go. The good news is that this quality does dissipate with time. The bad news is it may take 20 years for this to happen. You can speed this process along if you make a conscious attempt to do so. When you meet with success, remind yourself that it came from your efforts, your own hard work. Perhaps your luck or charm helped a little, but people who only have that going for them are found out relatively early. And always take time to enjoy your successes. Take your family out to dinner to celebrate. Write all the relatives and let them know what you have done. All too often, impostors view successes as not being successful enough. Don't do that to yourself. It can drive you crazy.

And if you have an occasional failure along the way (Susan and I both have had our share of them) do not, under any circumstances, view it as a sign from God that you are out of your league. If you never stumble, the chances are you are not stretching your abilities to their limits.

How Smart Are You About Taking Tests?

✓

THE TEST-WISENESS TEST

DIRECTIONS: This scale measures your test-taking ability. It consists of multiple-choice questions on history that you are *not* expected to know the answers to. However, all of the questions contain clues or hints that can permit the test-wise examinee to make intelligent guesses about the correct answers. Please read the questions carefully. There is only one correct answer for each question. There is no time limit for this test.

_____ 1. The Locarno Pact:
    a. is an international agreement for the maintenance of peace through the guarantee of national boundaries of France, Germany, Italy, Belgium, and other countries of Western Europe.
    b. allowed France to occupy the Ruhr Valley.
    c. provided for the dismemberment of Austria-Hungary.
    d. provided for the protection of Red Cross bases during wartime.

_____ 2. The disputed Hayes-Tilden election of 1876 was settled by an:
   a. resolution of the House of Representatives.
   b. decision of the United States.
   c. Electoral Commission.
   d. joint resolution of Congress.

_____ 3. The Factory Act of 1833 made new provisions for the inspection of the mills. This new arrangement was important because:
   a. the inspectors were not local men and therefore they had no local ties that might affect the carrying out of their jobs; they were responsible to the national government rather than to the local authorities, and they were encouraged to develop a professional skill in handling their work.
   b. the inspectorate was recruited from the factory workers.
   c. the inspectors were asked to recommend new legislation.
   d. the establishment of the factory inspectorate gave employment to large numbers of the educated middle class.

_____ 4. The Ostend Manifesto aimed to:
   a. discourage Southern expansionism.
   b. prevent expansion in the South.
   c. aid Southern expansionism.
   d. all of the above.

_____ 5. The august character of the work of Pericles in Athens frequently causes his work to be likened to that in Rome of:
   a. Augustus.
   b. Sulia.
   c. Pompey.
   d. Claudius.

_____ 6. One of the main reasons for the breakup of the Dual Monarchy was:
a. the speech defect of Emperor Francis Joseph.
b. the conflict of nationalities.
c. the defeat of the Chinese.
d. the Bolshevist revolution.

_____ 7. The Webster-Ashburton Treaty settled a long-standing dispute between Great Britain and the United States over:
a. the Maine boundary.
b. numerous contested claims to property as well as many other sources of ill will.
c. damages growing out of the War of 1812 and subsequent events.
d. fishing rights on the Great Lakes and in international waters.

_____ 8. The father of international law was:
a. Justinian and Possidon.
b. the British jurists.
c. the Papal juridical delegates.
d. Grotius.

_____ 9. Men who opposed the "Ten Hour Movement" in British factory history:
a. was a leader in the dominant political party.
b. is convinced that shorter hours of work are bad for the morals of the laboring classes.
c. is primarily motivated by concern for his own profits.
d. were convinced that intervention would endanger the economic welfare of Britain.

_____10. Roman imperialism affected landholding by:
    a increasing the number of small farms.
    b. eliminating farming in favor of importing all foodstuffs.
    c. bringing about a more democratic division of land.
    d. increasing the number of large estates and reducing the number of small farms, thereby increasing the number of landless persons.

_____11. The Declaration of the Rights of Man was:
    a. adopted by the French National Assembly.
    b. adopted by every Western European legislature.
    c. immediately ratified by every nation in the world.
    d. hailed by every person in England.

_____12. If you consider what Augustus says in *Monumentum Ancyranum* as stating what he really believes, with which of the following views do you think he would agree?
    a. the view that the senate should be abolished.
    b. the view that Augustus brought back the original and ancient form of the Republic.
    c. the view that there remained some shadow of the Republic.
    d. the view that the principate was a monarchy.

_____13. The U.S. Department of Agriculture removed all controls over cotton acreage for 1951 because:
   a. cotton had become totally worthless commercially with the introduction and wide use of rayon and nylon.
   b. the boll weevil had destroyed the entire cotton crop in all three previous years and had created a nationwide shortage of cotton.
   c. total cessation of German and Japanese cotton production since World War II had created a world cotton shortage.
   d. the use of cotton had increased and the cotton surplus had declined.

_____14. The career of Marius (157–86 B.C.), the opponent of Sulia, is significant in Roman history because:
   a. he gave many outstanding dinners and entertainments for royalty.
   b. he succeeded in arming the gladiators.
   c. he showed that the civil authority could be thrust aside by the military.
   d. he made it possible for the popular party to conduct party rallies outside the city of Rome.

_____15. The Locarno Pact:
   a. was an agreement between Greece and Turkey.
   b. gave the Tyrol to Italy.
   c. was a conspiracy to blow up the League of Nations building at Locarno.
   d. guaranteed the boundary arrangements in Western Europe.

_____16. Horace in the 16th Epode emphasizes the:
   a. despair of the average man confronted by sweeping social change.
   b. elation of the average man confronted by sweeping social change.
   c. optimism of the common man about sweeping social change.
   d. all of the above.

_____17. The wars that Thucydides, the historian, wrote a history of were:
   a. the Peloponnesian Wars.
   b. the Persian War.
   c. the March of the Ten Thousand.
   d. the conquest of Egypt by Alexander the Great.

_____18. The first presidential election dispute in the United States to be settled by an appointed Electoral Commission was:
   a. the Hayes-Tilden election.
   b. the Jefferson-Madison election.
   c. the John Quincy Adams-Henry Clay election.
   d. the Garfield-McKinley election.

_____19. The first great written code of laws was:
   a. Civilia Equus.
   b. Corpus Juris Civilia.
   c. Hammurabi's Codus Juris.
   d. Draco's Juris Categorus.

_____20. The first of the alliances against the "Central Powers" that ended in World War I is to be found in:
   a. the defensive treaty between China and Japan.
   b. the dual alliance of Mexico and the United States.
   c. the dual alliance of France and Russia.
   d. India's resentment against South Africa's attitude toward the Boer War, and her ensuing alliance with Japan.

_____21. The mercantilists believed in:
   a. expansion of Federal powers.
   b. merchant control of colonies.
   c. an income tax.
   d. organized trade unions.

_____22. The Proclamation of 1763:
   a. forbade colonists to settle territory acquired in the French and Indian wars.
   b. encouraged colonists to settle territory acquired in the French and Indian Wars.
   c. provided financial incentives for settlement of territory acquired in the French and Indian wars.
   d. all of the above.

_____23. About what fraction of the 1920 population of the United States was foreign-born?
   a. less than 5%.
   b. between 14% and 28%.
   c. 25%.
   d. between 30% and 50%.

_____24. In Roman history, a very famous political controversy developed around the relative power of the civil as opposed to the military components of government. Sulia defended the position that the civil authority was supreme. His opponent, who favored military authority, was:
   a. Marius.
   b. Cicero.
   c. Phidias.
   d. Polybius.

_____25. The Alabama claims were:
   a. all settled completely and satisfactorily.
   b. claims against Jefferson Davis for seizure of all of the property in the state during wartime.
   c. claims of the United States against Great Britain.
   d. claims of every citizen of Alabama against every citizen of Georgia.

_____26. During the Italian Renaissance:
   a. the papacy gained political power.
   b. there were frequent changes in government.
   c. the papacy became more important in Italian political affairs.
   d. all of the above.

_____27. Emperor Frederick II in his appeal to the kings of Europe:
   a. vehemently attacked European patriotism.
   b. argued that European patriotism belonged to the 12th century and was outmoded.
   c. argued strongly against the revival of European patriotism.
   d. all of the above.

_____28. The author of *Monumentum Ancyranum* was:
   a. Vellcius Paterculus.
   b. Tacitus.
   c. Strabo.
   d. Augustus.

_____29. The 12th century was distinguished by a "real European patriotism" that expressed itself in:
   a. the flowering of lyrical and epical poetry in the vernacular.
   b. great patriotic loyalty to the undivided unit of European Christendom.
   c. recurring attempts to form a world with a centralized administration.
   d. proposal to remove the custom barriers between the different countries of the time.

_____30. The dispute between Great Britain and the United States over the boundary of Maine was settled by:
   a. the Treaty of Quebec.
   b. the Treaty of Niagara.
   c. the Webster-Ashburton Treaty.
   d. the Pendleton-Scott Treaty.

_____31. In the *Dartmouth College* case the United States Supreme Court held:
   a. that the courts had no right under any circumstances ever to nullify an Act of Congress.
   b. that a state could not impair a contract.
   c. that all contracts must be agreeable to the state legislature.
   d. that all contracts must inevitably be certified.

_____32. The accession of Henry VII marked the close of the:
   a. Crusades.
   b. War of the Roses, between rival factions of the English nobility.
   c. Hundred Years' War.
   d. Peasants' Revolt.

_____33. The Magna Carta was signed:
   a. before the Norman invasion.
   b. in 1215.
   c. after the opening of the 17th century.
   d. about the middle of the 14th century.

_____34. The Progressive Party in 1912:
   a. favored complete protective tariffs.
   b. favored an appointed Congress.
   c. favored the creation of a nonpartisan tariff commission.
   d. favored restriction of the ballot to certain influential persons.

_____35. The expressions "Cavaliers" and "Roundheads" came into use during the struggle between:
    a. Lincoln and the Congress.
    b. Charles I and Parliament.
    c. the American colonies and Canada.
    d. the Protestants and the Jews.

_____36. The Scalawags were:
    a. selfish Southern politicians who were members of the Republican party during the period of the Reconstruction.
    b. Northerners with Southern sympathies.
    c. Negroes.
    d. poor whites serving jail sentences.

_____37. The first systematic attempt to establish the Alexandrian synthesis between Christian religious belief and Greek civilization was undertaken at:
    a. Rome.
    b. Alexandria.
    c. Athens.
    d. Jerusalem.

_____38. The directory:
    a. governed France from 1795 to 1799.
    b. was overthrown in the 19th century.
    c. was the only honest government France has had.
    d. was established after the Crimean War.

_____39. The Bland-Allison Act:
    a. made all forms of money redeemable in silver.
    b. standardized all gold dollars in terms of silver and copper.
    c. made none of the paper money redeemable in silver.
    d. directed the Treasury Department to purchase a certain amount of silver bullion each month.

_____40. The famed Bayeaux Tapestry is a:
a. enormous re-creation of the Magna Carta scene.
b. extremely large impression of the Edict of Nantes.
c. immense picture of the Battle of Tours.
d. large representation of the Norman Conquest of England.

SOURCE: Wayne Weiten. "The TWT: A scale to measure test-wiseness on multiple-choice exams with adults." Unpublished manuscript, 1984. College of DuPage. Used by permission.
Dr. Weiten is currently at Santa Clara University, Santa Clara, California.

SCORING KEY FOR THE TEST-WISENESS TEST

1. a	15. d	28. d
2. c	16. a	29. b
3. a	17. a	30. c
4. c	18. a	31. b
5. a	19. c	32. b
6. b	20. c	33. b
7. a	21. b	34. c
8. d	22. a	35. b
9. d	23. c	36. a
10. d	24. a	37. b
11. a	25. c	38. a
12. b	26. d	39. d
13. d	27. d	40. d
14. c		

HOW DO YOU COMPARE?

SCORE	PERCENTILE
15	15
18	30
22	50
25	70
28	85

About Test-Wiseness

It begins early in life, this business of taking tests. Within a few months of learning to read that literary classic, *See Dick and Jane,* and learning to add two plus three, we are tested on our level of mastery. The pace of test-taking only increases as we proceed through school with more and more classroom tests as the number of subjects we take increases, along with a variety of standardized achievement tests thrown in (presumably to double-check our teachers' classroom tests). Just when we reach the point when we are good and sick of taking tests, we are faced with the most dreaded of all tests, the SAT. It has the power to determine how we will spend the next four years of our life. But even that's not the end of it. It can and does get worse. If you do manage to score reasonably well on the SAT and make it to college and if you are a glutton for punishment, you may decide to pursue graduate training. That's when the real horror begins. You must take the GRE, the LSAT, or the MCAT depending on your particular interest. These tests have the power to stop a majority of people dead in their tracks.

It's not even over when you finally get out of school. Medicine, real estate, insurance and social work are but a few of the occupations that require the passing of a licensure exam before they open their doors to practitioners. And even if you don't have to be licensed, there is a good chance the organization you work for—or want to work for—will require that you pass some sort of test before being hired or promoted. The tests never seem to end, so it will definitely pay you to sharpen your test-taking skills.

If you are like most people, you don't enjoy taking tests. And it's no wonder. Tests seem to erect barriers for more people than they open doors for. After all, only a small minority of your classmates will receive an A on the final exam. Even fewer will obtain SAT scores high enough to get them into Harvard. And fewer still will receive GRE or LSAT scores that will gain them admittance to the graduate school or law school of their choice. The fact of the matter is that we live in a highly competitive world, and more people are disappointed in their test scores than are pleased by them.

I don't know how many students I've heard say, over the years, something like, "These tests just aren't fair. I do well in my classes, and I know I could do well in medical school (or graduate school or law school) if I only had the chance. I'm just not good at taking tests." And they could be right. Test-taking is a skill, and Dr. Wayne Weiten has constructed this Test-Wiseness Scale to measure this skill. He has found that scores on this scale do correlate with performance on classroom tests, even when the influence of intelligence is factored out. The good news is that his research has shown that test-taking is a skill that can be learned with relatively brief training. If you did not score at the 85th percentile, you could learn something very important by carefully reading the following material.

People who construct tests know what the right answer is before they write the items. Often, without even realizing it, their knowledge of the right answer may cause them to provide clues to which alternative is correct. Researchers have identified eight common flaws that can help you to select the correct alternative even if you do not know anything about the subject. It is true that you are more likely to encounter these flaws on classroom-type tests and tests used in local settings than on tests that are used nationally, such as the SAT. At least some of the principles that Weiten has discussed, however, can be of help on most tests. The eight flaws are:

1. The incorrect options are highly implausible. This was true of items 6, 14, 20, 34, and 35. Take a look at item 14. No one would be remembered for his great parties for more than a few years, much less for 2000, so obviously "a" cannot be right. "b" is silly because gladiators are already armed or they wouldn't be gladiators. And "d" is foolish because popular parties can do pretty much what they want without anyone's advocacy. This leaves only "c" as a plausible response.

2. Equivalence and/or contradictions among options allow one to eliminate the incorrect options. This applies to items 4, 16, 22, 26, and 27. Let's apply this to item 4. We can eliminate alternatives "a" and "b" because they are equivalent while "d" could not be correct because it demands a contradiction. So "c" is the only possible answer.

3. Information in other items provides the answer. This provides the key for items 15, 18, 24, 28, and 30. Information provided in item 1, for instance, gives you the answer to item 15.

4. The correct option is more detailed or specific than the other alternatives. This is true for items 7, 12, 23, 33, and 38. This is a subtle one, but sometimes item writers will try to "dress up" the incorrect alternatives to make

them appear more plausible. The correct alternative is left to stand on its own merits.

5. The correct option is longer than all of the other options. See items 1, 3, 10, 32, and 36. Sometimes item-writers will spend so much effort eliminating any ambiguity from the correct alternative that they skimp on the incorrect ones.

6. There is a grammatical inconsistency between the stem and the incorrect options, but not the correct one. This is true for items 2, 8, 9, 17, and 40. This is probably the most obvious flaw, and hence the least common. But it may help you a few times.

7. The incorrect options include certain key words that tend to appear in false statements—words such as "every," "total," and "all." This is seen in items 11, 13, 25, 31, and 39. There are few absolutes in this world, so be wary of options that make it seem like one exists. They are likely to be incorrect.

8. There is a resemblance between the stem and the correct option, but not the incorrect options. See items 5, 19, 21, 29, and 37. Carelessness can cause item-writers to use similar, and sometimes even the same, words in the stem and the correct option.

One last piece of advice about test-taking: If you are like most people, you have heard the adage that your first impression is usually the correct one, so you should never change your answers. Well, it's not true. In a study of college student responses to classroom tests, it was found that students were almost three times as likely to change an incorrect answer to a correct one than a right answer to a wrong one (63% to 22%). Fifteen percent of the time they changed a wrong answer to another wrong answer.

These hints will be especially helpful to you if you are one of those people who seems to always be on the borderline. Being test-wise will not turn a dunce into a National Merit Scholar, but for those who score close to the cutoff point it can make the difference between being hired and being rejected, or between receiving that promotion and being passed over. Remember, even if you aren't familiar with the topic being addressed, you may find a clue to the right answer if you know what to look for. And even if you can eliminate only one or two incorrect alternatives, your odds of getting that passing score will definitely improve.

GETTING IT TOGETHER

This section will provide information that will tell you how well adjusted you are. After you complete the five following tests, you will know—

A. How comfortable you are with yourself.
B. Who you believe controls your fate.
C. How rational your view of the world is.
D. How much excitement you need in your life.
E. How much meaning you find in your life.

How Comfortable Are You With Yourself?

✓

THE SELF-ESTEEM INVENTORY

DIRECTIONS: Please mark each statement in the following way: If the statement describes how you usually feel, put a check in the column "Like Me." If the statement does not describe how you usually feel, put a check in the column "Unlike Me." There are no right or wrong answers. Read each statement quickly, and answer immediately "off the top of your head." Do not deliberate at length over each one.

LIKE ME   UNLIKE ME

_____   _____   1. I spend a lot of time daydreaming.

_____   _____   2. I'm pretty sure of myself.

_____   _____   3. I often wish I were someone else.

_____   _____   4. I'm easy to like.

_____   _____   5. My family and I have a lot of fun together.

_____   _____   6. I never worry about anything.

_____   _____   7. I find it very hard to talk in front of a group.

67

_____ _____ 8. I wish I were younger.

_____ _____ 9. There are lots of things about myself I'd change if I could.

_____ _____ 10. I can make up my mind without too much trouble.

_____ _____ 11. I'm a lot of fun to be with.

_____ _____ 12. I get upset easily at home.

_____ _____ 13. I always do the right thing.

_____ _____ 14. I'm proud of my work.

_____ _____ 15. Someone always has to tell me what to do.

_____ _____ 16. It takes me a long time to get used to anything new.

_____ _____ 17. I'm often sorry for the things I do.

_____ _____ 18. I'm popular with people my own age.

_____ _____ 19. My family usually considers my feelings.

_____ _____ 20. I'm never unhappy.

_____ _____ 21. I'm doing the best work that I can.

_____ _____ 22. I give in very easily.

_____ _____ 23. I can usually take care of myself.

_____ _____ 24. I'm pretty happy.

_____ _____ 25. I would rather associate with people younger than me.

_____ _____ 26. My family expects too much of me.

_____ _____ 27. I like everyone I know.

_____ _____ 28. I like to be called on when I am in a group.

_____ _____ 29. I understand myself.

_____ _____ 30. It's pretty tough to be me.

_____ _____ 31. Things are all mixed up in my life.

_____ _____ 32. People usually follow my ideas.

_____ _____ 33. No one pays much attention to me at home.

_____ _____ 34. I never get scolded.

_____ _____ 35. I'm not doing as well at work as I'd like to.

_____ _____ 36. I can make up my mind and stick to it.

_____ _____ 37. I really don't like being a man/woman.

_____ _____ 38. I have a low opinion of myself.

_____ _____ 39. I don't like to be with other people.

_____ _____ 40. There are many times when I'd like to leave home.

_____ _____ 41. I'm never shy.

_____ _____ 42. I often feel upset.

_____ _____ 43. I often feel ashamed of myself.

_____ _____ 44. I'm not as nice-looking as most people.

_____ _____ 45. If I have something to say, I usually say it.

_____ _____ 46. People pick on me very often.

_____ _____ 47. My family understands me.

_____ _____ 48. I always tell the truth.

_____ _____ 49. My employer or supervisor makes me feel I'm not good enough.

_____ _____ 50. I don't care what happens to me.

_____ _____ 51. I'm a failure.

_____ _____ 52. I get upset easily when I am scolded.

_____ _____ 53. Most people are better liked than I am.

_____ _____ 54. I usually feel as if my family is pushing me.

_____ _____ 55. I always know what to say to people.

_____ _____ 56. I often get discouraged.

_____ _____ 57. Things usually don't bother me.

_____ _____ 58. I can't be depended on.

SOURCE: Muriel B. Ryden. "An adult version of the Coopersmith Self-Esteem Inventory: Test-retest reliability and social desirability." *Psychological Reports,* 1978, *43,* 1189–1190. Used by permission. (Dr. Ryden's scale is a version of a scale developed by Dr. Stanley Coopersmith to measure self-esteem in children. Dr. Ryden's version is modified to be used with adults.)

SCORING KEY FOR THE SELF-ESTEEM INVENTORY

To find your score, count the number of times your responses agree with the keyed responses below. The majority of the items do measure self-esteem, but the eight items below that fall under the heading "The Lie Scale" were intended to identify people who were trying to present themselves in an unrealistically favorable light.

2. Like	22. Unlike	42. Unlike
3. Unlike	23. Like	43. Unlike
4. Like	24. Like	44. Unlike
5. Like	25. Unlike	45. Like
7. Unlike	26. Unlike	46. Unlike
8. Unlike	28. Like	47. Like
9. Unlike	29. Like	49. Unlike
10. Like	30. Unlike	50. Unlike
11. Like	31. Unlike	51. Unlike
12. Unlike	32. Like	52. Unlike
14. Like	33. Unlike	53. Unlike
15. Unlike	35. Unlike	54. Unlike
16. Unlike	36. Like	55. Like
17. Unlike	37. Unlike	56. Unlike
18. Like	38. Unlike	57. Like
19. Like	39. Unlike	58. Unlike
21. Like	40. Unlike	

The Lie Scale

The following eight items comprise the Lie Scale. To find your score, count the number of times your responses agree with the keyed responses below. If your score was three or higher, you may have been trying too hard to appear to have high self-esteem. You might want to take the test again with an eye toward being more honest with your-self.

1. Like	20. Like	41. Like
6. Like	27. Like	48. Like
13. Like	34. Like	

HOW DO YOU COMPARE?

SCORE		PERCENTILE
Men	*Women*	
33	32	15
36	35	30
40	39	50
44	43	70
47	46	85

Although psychologists continue to debate the issue of whether men and women really differ in their levels of self-esteem, the fact remains that women often score somewhat lower than men on tests such as this one. The reasons are unclear.

About Self-Esteem

To a large extent, research investigating self-esteem has been the victim of its own success. The degree to which we are comfortable with ourselves has been found to be related to so many other areas of psychological functioning that, for the most part, researchers have lost interest in self-esteem and have turned their attention toward the investigation of more specific personality variables. But the fact of the matter is, if you were asked to predict a person's behavior in as many situations as possible and you could only give that person one psychological test, his or her score on a measure of self-esteem might very well be the one piece of information you would want.

Self-esteem is related to overall adjustment, with those high in self-esteem having higher levels of overall adjustment than those low in self-esteem. More specifically, compared to those low in self-esteem, people with high scores on this measure are less anxious in a variety of situations, and they are less likely to be depressed, irritable, or aggressive. People low in self-esteem are more likely to have feelings of resentment, alienation, and unhappiness. Those low in self-esteem are also more likely to experience insomnia and psychosomatic symptoms.

Our self-esteem is especially likely to show itself in our relationships with other people. People who feel good about themselves tend to like others and to be accepting of their frailties. Because of their genuinely positive feelings toward and acceptance of others, these people tend to bring out the best in those around them. A cliche that contains more than a glimmer of truth is that a person who feels good about him- or herself makes other people feel good about themselves. Naturally, this aura makes these people quite appealing, and others tend to gravitate to them in both social and professional settings.

While we generally don't use the term self-esteem in our everyday conversations about people, we are all familiar with the concept of the inferiority complex—which can be thought of as extremely low self-esteem. Psychologist Don Hamachek, who wrote a wonderful book about self-esteem, has outlined seven signs of the inferiority complex. They are:

1. *Sensitivity to criticism.* Although people who feel inferior "know" they have shortcomings, they do not like other

people to point these out. They tend to perceive any form of criticism, regardless of how sensitively or constructively it is presented, as a personal attack. Pity the poor boss who has an employee with an inferiority complex.

2. *Inappropriate response to flattery.* This can work two ways. Some people are desperate to hear anything good about themselves and will be constantly fishing for compliments. Others may refuse to listen to anything positive about themselves because it is inconsistent with their own feelings.

3. *Hypercritical attitude.* People who do not feel good about themselves have trouble feeling good about anyone else. They look hard for the flaws and shortcomings of others to try to convince themselves that they really aren't so bad after all. These people cannot feel intelligent, attractive, competent, and so on, unless they are the *most* intelligent, attractive and competent person around.

4. *Tendency toward blaming.* Some people project their perceived weaknesses onto others in order to lessen the pain of feeling inferior. From here, it is only a short step to blaming others for one's failures.

5. *Feelings of persecution.* Carried to its extreme, blaming others can extend to believing that others are actively seeking to ruin you. If a man is fired from his job, for instance, it may comfort him to believe that his boss was out to get him. It allows him to avoid personal responsibility for his failure.

6. *Negative feelings about competition.* People who feel inferior like to win games and contests every bit as much as anyone else, but they tend to avoid such situations because

deep down, they believe they cannot win. And not coming in first is clear evidence of total failure.

7. *Tendency toward seclusiveness and timidity.* Because people with an inferiority complex believe that they are not as interesting or intelligent as others, they believe that other people will feel the same way about them. So they tend to avoid social situations, and when they are forced to be with others, they will avoid speaking up because they believe doing so will only provide an embarrassing demonstration of their dullness and stupidity. Whoever coined the expression "It is better to remain silent and be thought a fool than to speak up and remove all doubt" provided an apt description of those with an inferiority complex.

If you had an extremely high score on this scale, don't be too smug. There is some evidence that people with extremely high self-esteem may be that way as a result of defensive self-perceptions. We have all known people like this. These are the people who seem to exude self-confidence to the point of arrogance, but they show many of the signs of low self-esteem. They won't tolerate even a hint that they are less than perfect, they tend to be extremely critical of others, and they seem to have a need to prove to the rest of the world just how wonderful they are. It seems to be the case that people with moderately high self-esteem are the most well adjusted. Those with rigidly high self-esteem take themselves so seriously that they cannot tolerate any sign of potential weakness.

If you did score low on this scale, it does not mean that you are destined to a life of misery and self-doubt. First of all, keep in mind that this test, as well as all the others in this book, was designed to be used with a normal population. They were *not* intended to detect mental illness. Second, many people gradually become easier on themselves as they grow older after they learn from experience that they aren't so bad after all. You can help this process along by making a conscious effort to pat yourself on the back for the things you do well. Remember, you don't have to come in first to be proud of your efforts.

Who Controls Your Fate?

> ✓
> ## THE INTERNALITY, CHANCE, AND POWERFUL OTHERS SCALE

DIRECTIONS: Below is a series of attitude statements. Each represents a commonly held opinion. There are no right or wrong answers. You will probably agree with some items and disagree with others. Read each statement carefully. Then indicate the extent to which you agree or disagree by using the guidelines below. First impressions are usually best. Read each statement, decide if you agree or disagree and the strength of your opinion. Then write in the appropriate number.

1 = Strongly Disagree
2 = Disagree Somewhat
3 = Slightly Disagree
4 = Slightly Agree
5 = Agree Somewhat
6 = Strongly Agree

_____ 1. Whether or not I get to be a leader depends mostly on my ability.

_____ 2. To a great extent my life is controlled by accidental happenings.

77

_____ 3. I feel like what happens in my life is mostly determined by powerful people.

_____ 4. Whether or not I get into a car accident depends mostly on how good a driver I am.

_____ 5. When I make plans, I am almost certain to make them work.

_____ 6. Often there is no chance of protecting my personal interests from bad luck.

_____ 7. When I get what I want, it's usually because I'm lucky.

_____ 8. Although I might have good ability, I will not be given leadership responsibility without appealing to those in positions of power.

_____ 9. How many friends I have depends on how nice a person I am.

_____ 10. I have often found that what is going to happen will happen.

_____ 11. My life is chiefly controlled by powerful others.

_____ 12. Whether or not I get into a car accident is mostly a matter of luck.

_____ 13. People like myself have very little chance of protecting our personal interests when they conflict with those of strong pressure groups.

_____ 14. It's not always wise for me to plan too far ahead because many things turn out to be a matter of good or bad fortune.

_____ 15. Getting what I want requires pleasing those people above me.

_____16. Whether or not I get to be a leader depends on whether I'm lucky enough to be in the right place at the right time.

_____17. If important people were to decide they didn't like me, I probably wouldn't make many friends.

_____18. I can pretty much determine what will happen in my life.

_____19. I am usually able to protect my personal interests.

_____20. Whether or not I get into a car accident depends mostly on the other driver.

_____21. When I get what I want, it's usually because I worked hard for it.

_____22. In order to have my plans work, I make sure that they fit in with the desires of people who have power over me.

_____23. My life is determined by my own actions.

_____24. It's chiefly a matter of fate whether or not I have a few friends or many friends.

SOURCE: Hanna Levenson. "Distinctions within the concept of internal-external control: Development of a new scale." Paper presented at American Psychological Association, 1972. Used by permission.

SCORING KEY FOR
THE INTERNALITY, POWERFUL OTHERS, AND
CHANCE SCALES

As its name suggests, there are three subscales on this test—internality, powerful others, and chance. To find your score on the Internality subscale, add together your responses on items 1, 4, 5, 9, 18, 19, 21, and 23. Your score on the Powerful Others subscale is obtained by adding together your responses on items 3, 8, 11, 13, 15, 17, 20, and 22. And finally, your Chance score is found by adding together your responses for items 2, 6, 7, 10, 12, 14, 16, and 24.

A high score on the internality scale indicates a belief that one's efforts can make a difference in the outcome of events, a high score on the powerful others scale indicates a belief that one's fate is determined by "powerful others," and a high score on the chance scale indicates a belief that life events are determined by luck.

HOW DO YOU COMPARE?

	SCORE		PERCENTILE
	Men	*Women*	
Internality	26	26	15
	29	29	30
	32	32	50
	35	35	70
	38	38	85
Powerful Others	9	7	15
	13	10	30
	17	14	50
	21	18	70
	25	21	85

Chance	7	6	15
	11	10	30
	15	13	50
	19	16	70
	23	20	85

As you can see from the norms, men and women are very similar in terms of how much they believe their own efforts determine their fate, but men are more likely than women to believe that powerful others and chance influence their lives.

About Internality

Who controls your fate? Or to be more accurate, who do you *believe* controls your fate? That is the question that Levenson's Internality, Powerful Others, and Chance Scales answers. This test is actually a refinement of an existing personality scale developed by Julian Rotter called the Internal-External Locus of Control Scale. Let me tell you a little about internals and externals before returning to Levenson's version of this personality characteristic.

Rotter believed that one dimension along which people varied was the degree to which they believed they controlled what happened to them. Those who felt that their efforts made a difference; that is, as long as they tried they could get the job, the girl, or whatever it was that they were after, were labeled internals. People who believed that nothing they did made much of a difference, that they were pawns manipulated by fate, luck, or capricious powerful others, were called externals. Internals and externals differ in a number of important ways. Generally, internals are more active, alert, and task-oriented in their attempts to manipulate and control their world. Externals tend to feel that nothing they can do will make a difference. They have no choice but to sit back and take whatever fate hands to them. As an indication of how important this personality dimension can be, one study found that tuberculosis patients who were internals knew more about their condition, made more of an effort to maintain their health, and in fact were more successful in doing so than were patients who were externals. Levenson's scale is very similar to the original Internal-External Locus of Control Scale, except that she divides externals into two subgroups; those who believe their fate is controlled by powerful others and those who believe their fate is controlled by chance. Both of these subgroups have an external locus of control.

Externals, those with high scores on the Powerful Others and Chance subscales, have a tough time of it. They tend to be somewhat neurotic, resentful, suspicious of others, irritable, depressed, and low in self-esteem. This is not to say that internals cannot have their share of psychological problems because they certainly can, but externals do in fact tend to view the world as a threatening and hostile place, and they tend to feel that nothing they can do will make it better. It is indeed a frightening way to view life.

One interesting thing about internals and externals is that their locus of control can flip-flop under some circumstances. Imagine that you are asked to perform a task that you have little experience with—an anagram, for example. You are given a group of letters such as "odgo" and asked to rearrange them so they make a word. After you finish, you are told that you have a very high score. What do you say to yourself about your performance? Internals, who tend to be high in self-esteem, are likely to say something such as, "That doesn't surprise me, I'm an intelligent person and I'm good with words," or "Well, I tried really hard to do my best." Externals, on the other hand, are likely to say something like, "Well, it must have been an easy test," or "I must have been lucky." Externals can't seem to take credit for their successes.

But externals can take credit for their failures. Had they been told they had performed poorly on the task, they might have said, "Well, I'm not very smart about that sort of thing." Internals, on the other hand, make an exception to their typical locus of control when they fail. So an internal might say in response to being told that he or she had a low score on the task, "Well, it was too hard for anyone to do well on it," or "You didn't give me enough time." Consequently, internals tend to maintain their sense of mastery because they believe they are responsible for the good things that happen to them, while externals sink deeper and deeper into their sense of hopelessness about making anything good happen to them.

Another interesting consequence of this locus of control variable involves decision-making strategies. To illustrate, suppose Jim is footloose, fancy-free, and new in town and interested in meeting a few women to ease his transition to his new circumstances. He decides to go to a popular singles bar and try out his skills at meeting people. Three times he picks out an attractive target for his affections, walks up to her and says, "Hi, I'm Jim. What's your sign?" And three times he is told to get lost. If Jim is an internal, he is likely to take stock and change his strategy. He realizes that what he has been doing hasn't worked, and he needs to try something new. If Jim is an external, he may very well approach a fourth woman and once again ask, "What's your sign?"

Internals tend to stick with a winning strategy and change a losing one. Externals, on the other hand, are likely to change their strategy after they meet with success and stick with one after experiencing failure. It's as if they are saying to themselves, "Well, it didn't work this time.

I'm due for a change of luck." Externals have been described as subscribing to the gambler's fallacy. If they flip a
coin ten times in a row and it comes up heads every time,
they are convinced that the next toss will result in a tail.
Internals might wonder if there are heads on both sides of
the coin.

As is the case with most personality characteristics, internals and externals are trained to be the way they are while
they are growing up. It is always hard to change a lifetime
of training, so if you scored low on the Internality subscale
and high on the other two, it will take a considerable effort to change—but you can do it if you try! It is not a matter of luck or powerful people controlling the way you are.
If you find yourself thinking that nothing you can do will
improve your situation, stop yourself. Try to think about
other people who faced similar circumstances and were
able to make a difference by making an effort. Think
about specific strategies you could employ. Ask your
friends for advice about what you might do. Point out to
yourself every time your efforts do result in a favorable
outcome and remind yourself of these occasions frequently. The truth is that there are some things that we really cannot control, but it is also true that simply by
believing that our efforts will make a difference, we can
lead happier, more satisfying lives.

How Rational Is Your View of the World?

THE RATIONAL
BEHAVIOR INVENTORY

DIRECTIONS: For each of the following questions, please use the following guide to indicate which most clearly reflects your opinion. Work quickly and answer each question.

> 5 = Strongly Disagree
> 4 = Disagree
> 3 = Neutral
> 2 = Agree
> 1 = Strongly Agree

_____ 1. Helping others is the very basis of life.

_____ 2. It is necessary to be especially friendly to new colleagues and neighbors.

_____ 3. People should observe moral laws more strictly than they do.

_____ 4. I find it difficult to take criticism without feeling hurt.

_____ 5. I often spend more time trying to think of ways of getting out of things than it would take me to do them.

_____ 6. I tend to become terribly upset and miserable when things are not the way I would like them to be.

_____ 7. It is impossible at any given time to change one's emotions.

_____ 8. It is sinful to doubt the Bible.

_____ 9. Sympathy is the most beautiful human emotion.

_____10. I shrink from facing a crisis or difficulty.

_____11. I often get excited or upset when things go wrong.

_____12. One should rebel against doing things, however necessary, if doing them is unpleasant.

_____13. I get upset when neighbors are very harsh with their little children.

_____14. It is realistic to expect that there should be no incompatibility in marriage.

_____15. I frequently feel unhappy with my appearance.

_____16. A person should be thoroughly competent, adequate, talented, and intelligent in all possible respects.

_____17. What others think of you is most important.

_____18. Other people should make things easier for us, and help with life's difficulties.

_____19. I tend to look to others for the kind of behavior they approve as right or wrong.

_____20. I find that my occupation and social life tend to make me unhappy.

_____21. I usually try to avoid doing chores that I dislike doing.

_____22. Some of my family and/or friends have habits that bother and annoy me very much.

_____23. I tend to worry about possible accidents and disasters.

_____24. I like to bear responsibility alone.

_____25. I get terribly upset and miserable when things are not the way I like them to be.

_____26. I worry quite a bit over possible misfortunes.

_____27. Punishing oneself for all errors will prevent future mistakes.

_____28. One can best help others by criticizing them and sharply pointing out the error of their ways.

_____29. Worrying about a possible danger will help ward it off or decrease its effects.

_____30. I worry about little things.

_____31. Certain people are bad, wicked, or villainous and should be severely blamed and punished for their sins.

_____32. A large number of people are guilty of bad sexual conduct.

_____33. One should blame oneself severely for all mistakes and wrongdoings.

_____34. It makes me very uncomfortable to be different.

_____35. I worry over possible misfortunes.

_____36. I prefer to be independent of others in making decisions.

_____37. Because a certain thing once strongly affected one's life, it should indefinitely affect it.

SOURCE: Clayton T. Shorkey and Victor L. Whiteman. "Development of the rational behavior inventory: Initial validity and reliability." *Educational and Psychological Measurement,* 1977, *37,* 527–534. Used by permission.

SCORING KEY FOR THE
RATIONAL BEHAVIOR INVENTORY

The authors of this scale have developed what they call "cutting" scores. If the number you used for an item is equal to or greater than the cutting score, give yourself 1 point for that item. If the number you used is less than the cutting score, give yourself a 0 for that item. For example, if you used either a 4 or 5 for item 1, then you would give yourself 1 point for this item. If you used a 1, 2, or 3, then you would score this item as a 0. The cutting scores for the items are provided below:

1. 4	10. 3	19. 3
2. 4	11. 3	20. 3
3. 3	12. 3	21. 4
4. 4	13. 4	22. 4
5. 3	14. 3	23. 3
6. 3	15. 4	24. 4
7. 3	16. 4	25. 3
8. 3	17. 3	26. 3
9. 4	18. 3	27. 3

28. 3		32. 3		35. 3
29. 3		33. 3		36. 3
30. 4		34. 3		37. 3
31. 4				

There is one last thing you must do before calculating your total score. Items 24 and 36 are reverse scored, so if you gave yourself a 1 for either of these items, change it to a 0. If you gave yourself a 0, change it to a 1. After doing this, add all the 1's together for your final score.

HOW DO YOU COMPARE?

SCORE	PERCENTILE
22	15
24	30
26	50
28	70
30	85

People with high scores on this scale are likely to be rational and logical in their view of the world. People with low scores are likely to accept a variety of assertions from others uncritically.

About Rational Behavior

The Rational Behavior Inventory was constructed to be used by psychotherapists to assess the rationality of their clients' behavior. It was inspired by a particular brand of psychotherapy; namely, Rational Emotive Therapy as developed by Albert Ellis. Ellis believes that people have problems because they are illogical or irrational, and the goal of therapy is to help people give up their old, irrational ways of viewing the world and to adopt a more rational, scientific approach to life.

To illustrate, imagine a man who came into therapy because he was depressed. The therapist would ask why and the man might reply, "I'm depressed because my wife left me." To cut right to the heart of the matter, the therapist would say something like, "You're not depressed because your wife left you, you're depressed because of the things you're telling yourself about your wife leaving. You're telling yourself that it's terrible that your wife left you, that it proves that you're a failure as a man and as a husband." The client would probably object at first, but the therapist's point would be that people do not have emotional reactions because of the things that happen to them. Their emotional reactions result from the thoughts they have about the things that happen to them. Because the client was depressed, he had to be telling himself irrational, illogical things about his wife leaving.

In this situation, it would be the therapist's job to teach the client to have more rational and logical thoughts about his wife's leaving. The client might be instructed to tell himself, "It's too bad my wife left me. I really was very attached to her. But there are lots of other women out there that I could also love, and they might be able to appreciate my good qualities. And besides, my wife's leaving me is a good opportunity to take a close look at myself so my next relationship can be more successful."

Ellis believes nothing that happens to us is catastrophic or horrible. Lots of things that happen are "too bad" or "unfortunate," but we experience anxiety and depression only because we convince ourselves that these "unfortunate" events are catastrophic.

Ellis has identified a number of irrational ideas that he believes are especially likely to be associated with psychological distress, and the items on the Rational Behavior Inventory reflect these ideas. Some examples of these beliefs are as follows:

1. One *must* have the love and approval of everyone important in one's life.
2. One must be thoroughly competent, adequate, and achieving in everything one does.
3. People who mistreat you are bad, wicked, or villainous and deserve to be severely punished.
4. It is not possible to control one's feelings when bad things happen.
5. When something is dangerous or frightening, one must become preoccupied and upset about it.
6. It is easier to avoid than to face life's difficulties.
7. One's life is determined by one's past, and it is impossible to do anything to change this.
8. All problems have good solutions.

Ellis's brand of psychotherapy may not be for everyone, but it does work. Several studies have found that people with neurotic impairments do improve after a course of Rational Emotive Therapy.

While Ellis's techniques may be effective, his assumptions have been questioned by his colleagues. To repeat, Ellis believes that people would be happier if they were more rational and logical in their thinking, but the truth is many happy and productive people can be quite irrational and illogical. Therapists have provided numerous examples where people's illusions may be the very thing that keeps them going. For instance, I know a young woman who has a disease that has a high probability of resulting in her death in a few years, but she continues to function effectively as a wife and a mother. She has times when she feels quite depressed, but for the most part she finds joy in her day-to-day activities. Her belief that her treatments will work, that she will be able to lick her illness, is what keeps her going. It may not be rational or logical to have such beliefs, but they certainly help to improve the quality of the time she does have. Indeed, there are a few studies that show that depressed people have fewer distortions than happy people. Perhaps we all have to have at least a few illusions to keep us going.

Having said that, I do like Ellis's approach and have used it myself in clinical practice. But it is important to keep in mind that the items on the Rational Behavior Inventory do reflect a philosophy and not some absolute truth about the best way to live. If you have problems with depression or anxiety and you received a score below the fiftieth percentile, you may find it useful to use this test as a vehicle for examining your own beliefs. But if you are basically happy with your life, you are certainly capable of developing your own philosophy of life.

How Much Excitement Do You Need in Your Life?

> ✓
>
> ## SENSATION-SEEKING SCALE— FORM V

DIRECTIONS: Each of the items below contains two choices, A and B. Please circle the choice that more closely describes your likes or the way you feel.

1. A. I like wild, uninhibited parties.
   B. I prefer quiet parties with good conversation.

2. A. There are some movies I enjoy seeing a second or even a third time.
   B. I can't stand watching a movie that I've seen before.

3. A. I often wish I could be a mountain climber.
   B. I can't understand people who risk their necks climbing mountains.

4. A. I dislike all body odors.
   B. I like some of the earthy body smells.

5. A. I get bored seeing the same old faces.
   B. I like the comfortable familiarity of everyday friends.

6. A. I like to explore a strange city or section of town by myself, even if it means getting lost.

   B. I prefer a guide when I am in a place I don't know well.

7. A. I dislike people who do or say things just to shock or upset others.

   B. When you can predict almost everything a person will do and say, he or she must be a bore.

8. A. I usually don't enjoy a movie or play when I can predict what will happen in advance.

   B. I don't mind watching a movie or play when I can predict what will happen in advance.

9. A. I have tried marijuana or would like to.

   B. I would never smoke marijuana.

10. A. I would not like to try any drug that might produce strange and dangerous effects on me.

    B. I would like to try some of the new drugs that produce hallucinations.

11. A. A sensible person avoids activities that are dangerous.

    B. I sometimes like to do things that are a little frightening.

12. A. I dislike swingers (people who are uninhibited and free about sex).

    B. I enjoy the company of swingers.

13. A. I find that stimulants make me uncomfortable.

    B. I often like to get high (drinking alcohol or smoking marijuana).

14. A. I like to try new foods that I have never tasted before.
    B. I order the dishes with which I am familiar so as to avoid disappointment and unpleasantness.

15. A. I enjoy looking at home movies or travel slides.
    B. Looking at someone's home movies or travel slides bores me tremendously.

16. A. I would like to take up the sport of water skiing.
    B. I would not like to take up water skiing.

17. A. I would like to try surfboard riding.
    B. I would not like to try surfboard riding.

18. A. I would like to take off on a trip with no preplanned or definite routes or timetable.
    B. When I go on a trip I like to plan my route and timetable fairly carefully.

19. A. I prefer the down-to-earth kinds of people as friends.
    B. I would like to make friends in some of the "far out" groups such as artists or "punks."

20. A. I would not like to learn to fly an airplane.
    B. I would like to learn to fly an airplane.

21. A. I prefer the surface of the water to the depths.
    B. I would like to go scuba diving.

22. A. I would like to meet some persons who are homosexual (men or women).
    B. I stay away from anyone I suspect of being gay or lesbian.

23. A. I would like to try parachute jumping.
    B. I would never want to try jumping out of a plane with or without a parachute.

24. A. I prefer friends who are excitingly unpredictable.
    B. I prefer friends who are reliable and predictable.

25. A. I am not interested in experience for its own sake.
    B. I like to have new and exciting experiences and sensations even if they are a little frightening, unconventional, or illegal.

26. A. The essence of good art is in its clarity, symmetry of form, and harmony of colors.
    B. I often find beauty in the "clashing" colors and irregular forms of modern paintings.

27. A. I enjoy spending time in the familiar surroundings of home.
    B. I get very restless if I have to stay around home for any length of time.

28. A. I like to dive off the high board.
    B. I don't like the feeling I get standing on the high board (or I don't go near it at all).

29. A. I like to date members of the opposite sex who are physically exciting.
    B. I like to date members of the opposite sex who share my values.

30. A. Heavy drinking usually ruins a party because some people get loud and boisterous.
    B. Keeping the drinks full is the key to a good party.

31. A. The worst social sin is to be rude.
    B. The worst social sin is to be a bore.

32. A. A person should have considerable sexual experience before marriage.
    B. It's better if two married persons begin their sexual experience with each other.

33. A. Even if I had the money, I would not care to associate with flighty rich persons such as those in the
jet set.
    B. I could conceive of myself seeking pleasure
around the world with the jet set.

34. A. I like people who are sharp and witty, even if they
do sometimes insult others.
    B. I dislike people who have their fun at the expense
of hurting the feelings of others.

35. A. There is altogether too much portrayal of sex in
movies.
    B. I enjoy watching many of the sexy scenes in
movies.

36. A. I feel best after taking a couple of drinks.
    B. Something is wrong with people who need liquor
to feel good.

37. A. People should dress according to some standard
of taste, neatness, and style.
    B. People should dress in individual ways even if
the effects are sometimes strange.

38. A. Sailing a long distance in a small sailing craft is
foolhardy.
    B. I would like to sail a long distance in a small but
seaworthy sailing craft.

39. A. I have no patience with dull or boring persons.
    B. I find something interesting in almost every per-
son I talk to.

40. A. Skiing down a high mountain slope is a good way
to end up on crutches.
    B. I think I would enjoy the sensation of skiing very
fast down a high mountain slope.

Reprinted with permission of Marvin Zuckerman. For more information, see: Marvin Zuckerman. *Behavioral Expressions and Biosocial Bases of Sensation Seeking*. New York: Cambridge University Press, 1994.

SCORING KEY

There are four subscales on the Sensation-Seeking Scale, each consisting of ten items. The subscales are: (1) *Thrill and Adventure Seeking* (TAS), (2) *Experience Seeking* (ES), (3) *Disinhibition* (DIS) and (4) *Boredom Susceptibility* (BS). To find your score on each subscale, add the number of times your response agrees with the scoring key below.

TAS	ES	DIS	BS
3. A	4. B	1. A	2. B
11. B	6. A	12. B	5. A
16. A	9. A	13. B	7. B
17. A	10. B	25. B	8. A
20. B	14. A	29. A	15. B
21. B	18. A	30. B	24. A
23. A	19. B	32. A	27. B
28. A	22. A	33. B	31. B
38. B	26. B	35. B	34. A
40. B	37. B	36. A	39. A

After you have found your four subscale scores, you can add them together for a total Sensation-Seeking score.

HOW DO YOU COMPARE?

The table below allows you to convert your score on each of the four subscales as well as your total Sensation-Seeking score into a percentile score. Notice that the norms are slightly different for men (M) and women (W), so find your raw score in the appropriate column and move to the far right of the table to find your percentile score.

TAS		ES		DIS		BS		TOTAL		PERCENTILE
M	W	M	W	M	W	M	W	M	W	
5	4	3	3	4	3	2	1	17	13	15
7	5	4	4	5	4	3	2	20	17	30
8	7	5	5	6	5	4	3	23	20	50
9	8	6	6	8	7	5	4	26	24	70
10	9	7	7	9	8	6	5	28	27	85

About Sensation-Seeking

Marvin Zuckerman of the University of Delaware has spent more than twenty years researching the personality trait he has come to call "Sensation-Seeking." His work, in my mind among the most fascinating in psychology, indicates that sensation-seeking is one of a handful of "core traits" that can be used to describe human personality. Furthermore, he presents convincing evidence that this characteristic has a strong genetic component—nearly as strong as that for intelligence. So, sensation-seeking parents are likely to have sensation-seeking children.

As you can see from scoring the test, sensation-seeking can be subdivided into the traits of Thrill and Adventure Seeking, Experience Seeking, Disinhibition, and Boredom Susceptibility. Thrill and Adventure Seeking is fairly self-explanatory. People who score high on this subscale enjoy activities that may entail some physical risk, such as rock climbing, skydiving, or white-water rafting. High scorers on the Experience Seeking subscale seek out novel experiences even if they do not involve excitement or danger. For instance, they are especially likely to volunteer for an experiment on meditation or hypnosis simply because they haven't done such things before. These people are also likely to prefer to try a new vacation spot each year rather than go back to the same old place regardless of how great it is. And they are likely to have more sexual partners than individuals low on the Experience Seeking scale. Disinhibition refers to the tendency to be open to experiences that may be unconventional or even illegal. Hence, as the items on this scale suggest, people with high scores are likely to enjoy heavy drinking at wild parties. They would be open to the possibility of spouse-swapping or illicit drug use. These people do not feel bound by conventional standards of morality. And finally, Boredom Susceptibility is self-explanatory. Such individuals find the ordinary and expected downright painful. The routines that most of us develop and find comfortable are an anathema to these people. They can become quite agitated and distressed if they cannot satisfy their needs for novelty.

Sensation-seeking has its advantages and disadvantages. People such as Christopher Columbus and Neil Armstrong were undoubtedly high in this trait. Sensation-seekers are the ones who are likely to make new discoveries or break new ground. They are not afraid to try something new and different. On the other hand, if they cannot channel their energies into socially acceptable ways, their tendencies may get them into trouble. Sensation-seeking can be a double-edged sword.

Because this characteristic is relatively fixed, Zuckerman has suggested that people should take their style into account when making certain life choices. When choosing a spouse, for instance, it would not be wise for an extreme sensation-seeker to marry someone who is at the other end of the continuum. These two people simply would not be able to appreciate each other. Vocational choice would be a second important consideration. A person low in sensation-seeking may enjoy the job of college professor, for example, since it is relatively secure and it can be gratifying. A person high in sensation-seeking would find the routine of such a job to be stultifying. The type of job that could keep a sensation-seeker interested, perhaps that of a real estate developer, probably would be much too stressful for the individual low in sensation-seeking. After finding your score, you may want to examine your life choices in relation to this very important, basic dimension of personality.

How Meaningful Is Your Life?

✓

THE EXISTENTIAL ANXIETY SCALE

DIRECTIONS: For the following items, if the statement describes how you feel or what you believe, respond with a T. If it does not describe how you feel or what you believe, respond with an F.

_____ 1. I frequently have the feeling that my life has little or no purpose.

_____ 2. I mostly feel bored and indifferent by what is going on around me.

_____ 3. I find life exciting and challenging.

_____ 4. I often feel that my accomplishments are pretty worthless.

_____ 5. I usually feel that I am merely existing, not really living.

_____ 6. I generally feel that it is useless to discuss things with others because they never really understand.

_____ 7. I feel that I have more to look forward to in life than most others do.

_____ 8. My daily activities mostly seem to be rather pointless.

_____ 9. I generally feel depressed when I think about the future.

_____10. I have never found any type of work that I really enjoy.

_____11. My feelings don't seem to mean anything to anyone else.

_____12. I find religion to be rather empty.

_____13. I feel that it is useless to try to convince anyone else of anything.

_____14. I often feel that I have little to look forward to.

_____15. I do not feel that life is meaningless.

_____16. I never seem to enjoy things the way others seem to.

_____17. I generally feel that I am getting nowhere, no matter how much effort I put forth.

_____18. I feel that I have found more meaning in life than most others have.

_____19. I rarely take a strong interest in what I am reading or studying.

_____20. There is nothing in my past life that is particularly worth remembering.

_____21. I feel that my life is of no real importance to anyone.

_____22. I can always find something to do that I really enjoy.

_____23. I feel that there is little, if anything, in this world that is particularly worth pursuing over a long period.

_____24. My life seems to be rather aimless.

_____25. I find it difficult to believe strongly in anything.

_____26. Almost everyone I know seems to live a rather empty life.

_____27. Generally, I feel that what I do is pretty useless.

_____28. I usually don't know what to do with myself.

_____29. I do not have any important goals in life.

_____30. I mostly feel all alone in the world.

_____31. I seldom feel a strong sense of responsibility for any other person.

_____32. I feel that I am a productive person.

SOURCE: Lawrence R. Good and Katherine C. Good. "A preliminary measure of existential anxiety." *Psychological Reports,* 1974, *34,* 72–74. Used by permission.

SCORING KEY

1. T	12. T	23. T
2. T	13. T	24. T
3. F	14. T	25. T
4. T	15. F	26. T
5. T	16. T	27. T
6. T	17. T	28. T
7. F	18. F	29. T
8. T	19. T	30. T
9. T	20. T	31. T
10. T	21. T	32. F
11. T	22. F	

HOW DO YOU COMPARE?

Score	Percentile
0	15
2	30
5	50
8	70
10	85

About Existential Anxiety

I confess to being a rather simple person. As long as my family is healthy and happy, as long as I have an interesting project to work on and I hit my fair share of good golf shots, and as long as my dog goes crazy with excitement when I get home, I'm happy. I haven't thought about the meaning of life or my place in the world since I was a sophomore in college. It's not that I found the answers. The questions simply lost their interest for me. I tell you this so you will understand why I have difficulty in grasping the concept of existential anxiety.

It certainly can be a problem for some people. While, as you can see from the norms, the average score on the Existential Anxiety Scale was only five, the authors reported that in their sample of about 200 people, some scores were as high as 26. In the words of Drs. Good and Good, existential anxiety is about despair, alienation, and emptiness, and there are people who do suffer from such feelings.

A number of mental health professionals sympathetic to existentialist philosophy have suggested reasons why such problems have become more common during the second half of the twentieth century. According to these writers, until World War II, the world was a relatively predictable place. People grew up in stable families, and they knew their lives would be similar to their parents'. Sure, each generation hoped to improve its lot, but people had a fairly clear sense of what their roles in the world would be. But change has been extremely rapid during the second half of this century. As existential psychologist James Bugental has pointed out, the 1950s brought the baby boom and the 1960s saw flower children. Next we had the hopeful 1970s, which mutated into the "Me Generation" of the 1980s. Now, in the 1990s, we have "Generation X." Bugental's point is that this rapid, sustained change in society has made it difficult for people to know what their place in it is. Our world has become undependable, and we must struggle to discover how we fit in.

Bugental agrees with other writers that people may have a predisposition to experience existential anxiety that can lie dormant for years, perhaps even a lifetime, and appear only under times of extraordinary stress. He described a young woman who was clearly the brightest person in her small high school. When she went to a prestigious university and discovered there were lots of people as bright as she was, her self-concept was shattered. She no longer knew where she fit in. Another case involved a woman who led a charmed life until her mid-30s. She was born to an affluent family and married a man from a similar background whom she dearly loved and who loved her. Her world was perfect—and dependable—until she lost her oldest child in an automobile accident. Her subsequent profound depression resulted not only from the loss of her child, but the resulting confrontation with her own vulnerability. She discovered that life was not always as easy as she had assumed.

Salvatore Maddi, one of the best known existential psychotherapists, has described the type of people who are likely to experience a bout of existential anxiety. Perhaps the best single word to describe such individuals is cynical.

These people believe that life is essentially meaningless and that nothing they do, or can even imagine themselves doing, has any inherent value or usefulness. Their predominant emotion is one of blandness. They may experience brief periods of depression—which become less frequent as they grow older—but mostly they feel emotionally numb. They have a definite inability to experience the pure joy of being alive that most of us occasionally experience in ordinary circumstances—such as while viewing a sunset or while watching children playing in the park. They tend to have a low energy level, but even more important, they have the sense that their activities are not freely chosen. They are doing what is expected of them, what they have to do to get by. Maddi believes there is a large number of such individuals in our society.

What should you do if you received a high score on the Existential Anxiety Scale, or if the above paragraph sounds all too familiar? That's the tough question. Unlike the practitioners of most other schools of therapy, existential therapists have not written self-help books for people who experience this problem. Indeed, Bugental has written that this form of psychotherapy is "lengthy, expensive, uncomfortable, and intrusive"—not encouraging words if you would like to find your place in the world.

There are two themes that run through these philosophers' works that may provide some guidance. First, they believe that healthy individuals focus on the abstract, the symbolic, and the imagined rather than the concrete or the material. Indeed, most of these writers point to our materialistic society as responsible for generating so many cases of existential anxiety (although one has to wonder why existential therapy is so expensive if its practitioners have such disdain for the material). Second, existential therapists speak of the importance of "awareness of immediate experience." I suspect I'm too "concrete" to fully understand what this means, but my sense is that they are saying that people should discover the value and importance of what they are doing at each particular moment. Too many of us live for the future. We tell ourselves we'll work hard now and when we finish school we'll begin to enjoy life. Then it becomes, "When I get that promotion and raise, I'll be happy," and then, "When we've saved enough for the kids' education." It will never end unless we decide to make each moment count. Life is to be lived, not planned for.

If I've sounded skeptical about existential anxiety (and I hope I have), it is because this approach represents a philosophy—not a scientific truth, as some of its practitioners would have us believe. Despite my skepticism, I do believe there is something to this concept. I think it can be seen most clearly in people whose apparent purpose in life is taken away from them. The successful executive, for instance, who becomes depressed upon retirement has never truly understood his place in the world. Or the star athlete who cannot cope when an injury ends his career. The ability to run fast while carrying a ball is not an adequate basis upon which to build a life. We are all well advised to take joy and find meaning in all of our activities, no matter how mundane.

SECTION III

GETTING ALONG

Humans are social animals, and if you are going to have a satisfying life, you have to have the qualities that make it easy for you to get to know others and to get along with them. This section will provide you with information about your interpersonal strengths and those areas that you might want to work on. After you complete the tests in this section, you will know—

A. How comfortable you are in social situations.
B. How assertive you are in your interpersonal relationships.
C. How dependent you are on others.
D. How competitive you are.
E. How argumentative you are.

How Comfortable Are You in Social Situations?

✓

THE SOCIAL INTERACTION SELF-STATEMENT TEST

DIRECTIONS: It is obvious that people think a variety of things when they are involved in different social situations. Below is a list of things you may have thought to yourself at some time before, during, or after an interaction in which you were engaged (with someone you would like to get to know). Read each item and decide how frequently you may have been thinking a similar thought before, during, or after the interaction.

Use a number from 1 to 5 for each item. The scale is interpreted as follows:

> 1 = *hardly ever* had the thought
> 2 = *rarely* had the thought
> 3 = *sometimes* had the thought
> 4 = *often* had the thought
> 5 = *very often* had the thought

Please answer as honestly as possible.

_____ 1. When I can't think of anything to say, I can feel myself getting very anxious.

_____ 2. I can usually talk to women/men pretty well.

_____ 3. I hope I don't make a fool of myself.

_____ 4. I'm beginning to feel more at ease.

_____ 5. I'm really afraid of what she'll/he'll think of me.

_____ 6. No worries, no fears, no anxieties.

_____ 7. I'm scared to death.

_____ 8. She/He probably won't be interested in me.

_____ 9. Maybe I can put her/him at ease by starting things going.

_____10. Instead of worrying, I can figure out how best to get to know her/him.

_____11. I'm not too comfortable meeting women/men, so things are bound to go wrong.

_____12. What the heck, the worst that can happen is that she/he won't go for me.

_____13. She/He may want to talk to me as much as I want to talk to her/him.

_____14. This will be a good opportunity.

_____15. If I blow this conversation, I'll really lose my confidence.

_____16. What I say will probably sound stupid.

_____17. What do I have to lose? It's worth a try.

_____18. This is an awkward situation, but I can handle it.

_____19. Wow—I don't want to do this.

_____20. It would crush me if she/he didn't respond to me.

_____21. I've just got to make a good impression on her/him, or I'll feel terrible.

_____22. You're such an inhibited idiot.

_____23. I'll probably bomb out anyway.

_____24. I can handle anything.

_____25. Even if things don't go well, it's no catastrophe.

_____26. I feel awkward and dumb; she's/he's bound to notice.

_____27. We probably have a lot in common.

_____28. Maybe we'll hit it off real well.

_____29. I wish I could leave and avoid the whole situation.

_____30. Ah! Throw caution to the wind.

SOURCE: Carol R. Glass, Thomas V. Merluzzi, Joan L. Biever, and Kathryn H. Larson. "The social interaction self-statement test." *Cognitive Therapy and Research*, 1982, 37–55. Used by permission.

SCORING KEY FOR THE SOCIAL INTERACTION SELF-STATEMENT TEST

Two scores are obtained for this test; a Positive Thoughts subscale and a Negative Thoughts subscale. For each subscale, simply add your numerical response for each of the 15 items appearing on the subscale.

Positive Thoughts	Negative Thoughts
2	1
4	3
6	5
9	7
10	8
12	11
13	15
14	16
17	19
18	20
24	21
25	22
27	23
28	26
30	29

HOW DO YOU COMPARE?

SISST Positive Thoughts

SCORE		PERCENTILE
Men	Women	
40	45	15
43	48	30
47	52	50
51	56	70
54	59	85

SISST Negative Thoughts

SCORE		PERCENTILE
Men	*Women*	
34	31	15
39	34	30
44	38	50
49	42	70
54	45	85

About Social Anxiety

"Better to remain silent and be thought a fool than to speak up and remove all doubt" is your credo if you had a high score on the Negative Thoughts portion of the Social Interaction Self-Statement Test. As is obvious from the items, people who receive high scores on this subscale tend to be nervous in social situations, and they make their nervousness worse by saying self-defeating things to themselves about their interactions with others. They are so convinced of their own social ineptitude that they approach every situation certain they will say something silly and that others will reject them.

A high score on the Positive Thoughts subscale, on the other hand, reflects people who have little anxiety in social situations and who believe themselves to be socially adept—which, in reality, they are. These people approach social situations with a positive attitude. They tell themselves that there is no need to be nervous, and even if they don't get the reaction they would like, it's no big deal. Their credo seems to be "Nothing ventured, nothing gained." It is much easier to approach strangers if you have this attitude.

You may have noticed that the norms for men and women are quite different. This reflects the fact that shyness (or social anxiety, to be faithful to psychological jargon) affects men and women differently. In a study of single adults I conducted a few years ago, I found that shy women had just as many social and dating relationships as did their non-shy counterparts. Shy men, on the other hand, were left out in the cold. They dated considerably less than non-shy men, and in general felt isolated and unhappy. Men still bear the brunt of responsibility of making the first move, so shy men, who are in the habit of telling themselves that women probably won't like them, have a difficult time meeting people. Women, who can be more passive and simply wait for a man to approach them, are not nearly as affected by their social insecurities.

If you scored at the 85th percentile or higher on the Negative Thoughts subscale, you are probably not enjoying your life as much as you might. You feel nervous and unsure of yourself, and your anxiety has cut you off from other people. You find it more comfortable to stay home alone than to put yourself in situations where others might reject you. It is not a very satisfying way to live.

The good news is that this is a problem that responds well to treatment, and you can set up your own program to feel more comfortable and relaxed around other people. Your goal should be to get out of the habit of saying things to yourself that appear on the Negative Thoughts subscale and get into the habit of telling yourself the things that are on the Positive Thoughts subscale. The key is to do it in small steps. Let me outline a simple, five-step program for you. You can, of course, improvise or add to it depending on your particular situation.

1. For the first two weeks, the only thing you have to do is to smile and say hello to strangers you make eye contact with—in appropriate situations, of course, which excludes

the subway in Manhattan. If you are taking college classes, smile and say hello to people who are entering the classroom with you. At work, smile and say hello to people who get on the elevator with you. Do it with the cashier when you buy gas or a newspaper. You are in the habit of waiting for others to initiate contact, but they don't know why you look so grim. You know that you don't feel confident and don't want to risk rejection, but they think you are standoffish and unapproachable. When you try this out, some people will look at you as if you are crazy, but don't let that stop you. Just repeat to yourself one of the Positive Thoughts. I think you will be surprised at how many people will respond with a friendly smile of their own, and before long it will seem more natural to say positive things to yourself.

2. During the second two-week segment, practice your small-talk skills. While you are waiting in line at the grocery store, turn to the person behind you and comment on what a beautiful day it is. When you pay for your gas, ask the cashier how she has been. You may wonder if such familiarity is appropriate, but your doubts are a result of your telling yourself that others will reject you. We have all seen people who seem to be the best of friends with the cashier at the grocery store when in reality they only see him or her once a week. You will meet exceptions, but a majority of people will respond to friendliness and openness in kind, and you need to remind yourself of this. And you will be surprised at how much nicer the world can seem if you have a relaxed, friendly relationship with people you don't really know but come in contact with frequently.

3. The third step of your self-treatment program is to offer other people compliments. You don't have to be gushy, but almost everyone likes to get a pat on the back every now and then. Tell your classmate that you thought

her comment was really good and made you think about the topic in a new way. Tell your coworker that you like his new tie. Tell your grocery store checker that she looks like she's feeling good today. One of the most basic principles of human relationships is that we like those who like us, so show other people you like them. They have probably assumed that your quietness reflects your lack of interest in them rather than your insecurities.

4. Step four is to begin reaching out; be the one who extends invitations. After completing the first three steps, you are feeling more comfortable around others and you are getting to know them. Now is the time to make new friends. Ask your coworker to have lunch with you. Ask your neighbor in for a beer. Ask your classmate to see a movie with you. Not everyone will say yes because not everyone will like you, but that is no excuse to stop trying. You don't like everyone you meet either. But if you are friendly and open, you will meet with more acceptances than rejections. Remember, nothing ventured, nothing gained.

5. Now that you are feeling more comfortable around individuals, it is time to face your apprehensions about being part of a larger group. You need practice, so you will have to find a group to join. Many colleges and continuing education programs do offer something perfect for you—assertiveness training groups. If you can find one of those, join it today. Toastmaster clubs and Dale Carnegie courses can provide you with similar opportunities. If you can't find anything like this, take an evening college class or join a book discussion club. Your task is to make at least one comment each meeting. At first you may have to prepare. You may want to write out your comment before the meeting and rehearse it in front of a mirror. You may feel nervous when you speak up the first time, but don't worry about it. The chances are that nobody else will notice. I

guarantee that it will get easier as you go along. Before long, you will find yourself wanting to speak up.

People with high Negative Thoughts scores do have one thing going for them—they take their obligations to others more seriously than those with low levels of social anxiety. This is probably true because they are worried about others thinking badly of them, but whatever the motive, it is a nice quality to have. Your concern about the reactions of others also makes you more sensitive than the average person. So you have the necessary ingredients to be a person who is liked and respected. All you have to do is let others know what is inside you.

Good luck. Keep trying until your Positive Thoughts score reaches the 85th percentile. I know you can do it.

How Assertive Are You?

> ## THE RATHUS ASSERTIVENESS SCHEDULE

DIRECTIONS: Indicate how uncharacteristic or descriptive each of the following statements is of you by using the code given below:

+3   very characteristic of me, extremely descriptive

+2   rather characteristic of me, quite descriptive

+1   somewhat characteristic of me, slightly descriptive

−1   somewhat uncharacteristic of me, slightly nondescriptive

−2   rather uncharacteristic of me, quite nondescriptive

−3   very uncharacteristic of me, extremely nondescriptive

_____ 1. Most people seem to be more aggressive and assertive than I am.

_____ 2. I have hesitated to make or accept dates because of shyness.

_____ 3. When the food served at a restaurant is not done to my satisfaction, I complain about it to the waiter or waitress.

_____ 4. I am careful to avoid hurting other people's feelings, even when I feel that I have been injured.

_____ 5. If a salesman has gone to considerable trouble to show me merchandise that is not quite suitable, I have a difficult time saying no.

_____ 6. When I am asked to do something, I insist upon knowing why.

_____ 7. There are times when I look for a good, vigorous argument.

_____ 8. I strive to get ahead as well as most people in my position.

_____ 9. To be honest, people often take advantage of me.

_____10. I enjoy starting conversations with new acquaintances and strangers.

_____11. I often don't know what to say to attractive persons of the opposite sex.

_____12. I hesitate to make phone calls to business establishments and institutions.

_____13. I would rather apply for a job or for admission to a college by writing letters than by going through with personal interviews.

_____14. I find it embarrassing to return merchandise.

_____15. If a close and respected relative were annoying me, I would smother my feelings rather than express my annoyance.

_____ 16. I have avoided asking questions for fear of sounding stupid.

_____ 17. During an argument I am sometimes afraid that I will get so upset that I will shake all over.

_____ 18. If a famed and respected lecturer makes a statement that I think is incorrect, I will have the audience hear my point of view as well.

_____ 19. I avoid arguing over prices with clerks and salesmen.

_____ 20. When I have done something important or worthwhile, I manage to let others know about it.

_____ 21. I am open and frank about my feelings.

_____ 22. If someone has been spreading false and bad stories about me, I see that person as soon as possible to have a talk about it.

_____ 23. I often have a hard time saying no.

_____ 24. I tend to bottle up my emotions rather than make a scene.

_____ 25. I complain about poor service in a restaurant or elsewhere.

_____ 26. When I am given a compliment, I sometimes just don't know what to say.

_____ 27. If a couple near me in a theater or at a lecture were conversing rather loudly, I would ask them to be quiet or to take their conversation elsewhere.

_____ 28. Anyone attempting to push ahead of me in a line is in for a good battle.

_____29. I am quick to express an opinion.

_____30. There are times when I just can't say anything.

SOURCE: Spencer A. Rathus. "A 30-item schedule for assessing assertive behavior." *Behavior Therapy,* 1973, *4,* 398–406. Used by permission.

SCORING KEY FOR THE RATHUS ASSERTIVENESS SCHEDULE

The first step to score this scale is to change the sign for the items that are reverse scored. For the items below, if you used a negative number, change the sign from a minus to a plus. If you used a positive number for these items, change the sign from a plus to a minus.

1	12	19
2	13	23
4	14	24
5	15	26
9	16	30
11	17	

After you have changed the signs for the items above, find your total score. If your math is a little rusty, you do this by adding together all the numbers with the same sign. You will end up with one positive and one negative number. Subtract the smaller number from the larger one and use the sign that was with the larger number.

HOW DO YOU COMPARE?

Score	Percentile
−29	15
−15	30
0	50
+15	70
+29	85

About Assertiveness

Assertiveness training was one of the first techniques developed by behavior therapists back in the late 1950s and early 1960s. By the late 1960s and early 1970s, when a large number of new clinical psychologists who had been trained in behavioral methods were beginning their practices, assertiveness training groups became ubiquitous. While they are not the fad now that they were two decades ago, anyone who is interested would have little difficulty in finding such a group in any but the remotest of locales. Are there really so many people who need to increase their assertiveness? Perhaps, but to at least some extent, the proliferation of assertiveness training experiences reflects the values of many mental health professionals.

If you received a score that was lower than the 15th percentile, you probably could benefit from becoming more assertive. The difficulty you have in speaking your mind is probably causing you to feel lonely, isolated, and exploited. But, on the other hand, I'm not so sure it should be your goal to have as high a score as possible. Contrary to what many other mental health professionals may tell you, I believe a medium level of assertiveness is perfectly acceptable. Extremely assertive individuals tend to be hard-driving, ambitious people who can also be self-centered. They have a tendency to believe that their own feelings and desires are more important than those of anyone else. Dr. Rathus provided some support for this position in his original research study with the scale. He found that people who had high scores on his scale were perceived by their close friends as not being as "nice" as those who were lower in assertiveness.

To be fair, there is an important distinction between assertiveness and aggressiveness. Assertiveness is defined as the socially appropriate expression of feelings, so assertive behavior need not be aggressive. Let's use one of the items on the Rathus Assertiveness Schedule as an example. Item 14 asks for feelings about returning merchandise. An aggressive person might complain loudly about the merchandise and belligerently demand a full refund. An assertive person would state the reasons for the return, not only in a clear and forthright fashion, but also calmly and reasonably, until a refund or credit was forthcoming. Assertive people are intent on making their feelings known to others. Aggressive people want to place themselves in a "one-up" position. This would be one situation where it would be desirable to be assertive.

To make my case that assertiveness need not always be the ideal, consider item 15, "If a close and respected relative were annoying me, I would smother my feelings rather than express my annoyance." I have my share of relatives who can be annoying, but I almost always smother my feelings. First of all, I see them, at most, a few times a year, so it's not as if I have to do much suffering in silence. Second, my relatives are who they are, and my expression of annoyance is not going to change them. They are not about to take my words of wisdom to heart and change their annoying ways. And third, I appreciate that I may have my own annoying ways and they are polite enough to keep their thoughts to themselves. There are some situations where it just isn't worth it to openly express all feelings.

If the Rathus Assertiveness Schedule does help you identify some situations that you could handle more effectively, it is possible to change your ways. As is the case with social anxiety discussed in the previous section, lack of assertiveness does respond well to treatment. Indeed, people with high levels of social anxiety tend to lack assertiveness. (However, not every one who is socially confident is assertive.) The same five-step program outlined in the previous section can help you become more assertive.

Because assertiveness, more so than social anxiety, tends to be related to specific situations, you may want to devise a somewhat more detailed plan for change. The first step is to list the situations in which you would like to be more assertive. You can use the items on the Rathus scale as a guide. Item 23, for instance, "I often have a hard time saying no," is a common problem for people low in assertiveness. If this is a problem for you, you might find it helpful to make a list of the situations in which you have trouble saying no even when you would like to.

The second step is to order this list in terms of how difficult each situation is for you. It may not be all that difficult for you to say no to a telephone caller soliciting for a charity, while it may be extremely difficult for you to say no to a close friend who asks to borrow your car. For each situation think of, or better yet, write down an assertive response that you believe is appropriate for the situation. To the telephone caller you might say, "I'm sorry I can't help you. My policy is never to send money in response to phone solicitations." To your friend you might simply say, "I don't lend my car to other people." In thinking about assertive responses, keep in mind that you do not have to explain your feelings, nor do you have to apologize for them. It is always nice to be tactful, but don't forget that it is the other person who is putting you on the spot by making an unreasonable request.

The third step is practice. Begin with the easiest tasks on your list, and as you begin to feel more comfortable with those, move up the hierarchy. Remember to use the techniques discussed in the previous section. When you are asserting yourself, catch yourself when you have negative thoughts and make a conscious effort to substitute positive thoughts. Practice may not make perfect, but it can make a difference. And remember, your goal is not to become a self-centered, aggressive person; you simply want to enjoy your social relationships and to keep others from taking advantage of you.

How Dependent Are You?

THE INTERPERSONAL DEPENDENCY INVENTORY

DIRECTIONS: 48 statements are presented below. Please read each one and decide whether or not it is characteristic of your attitudes, feelings or behavior. Then assign a rating to every statement, using the values given below.

> 4 = Very characteristic of me
> 3 = Quite characteristic of me
> 2 = Somewhat characteristic of me
> 1 = Not characteristic of me

_____ 1. I prefer to be by myself.

_____ 2. When I have a decision to make, I always ask for advice.

_____ 3. I do my best work when I know it will be appreciated.

_____ 4. I can't stand being fussed over when I am sick.

_____ 5. I would rather be a follower than a leader.

_____ 6. I believe people could do a lot more for me if they wanted to.

128

_____ 7. As a child, pleasing my parents was very important to me.

_____ 8. I don't need other people to make me feel good.

_____ 9. Disapproval by someone I care about is very painful for me.

_____10. I feel confident of my ability to deal with most of the personal problems I am likely to meet in life.

_____11. I'm the only person I want to please.

_____12. The idea of losing a close friend is terrifying to me.

_____13. I am quick to agree with the opinions expressed by others.

_____14. I rely on myself.

_____15. I would be completely lost if I didn't have someone special.

_____16. I get upset when someone discovers a mistake I have made.

_____17. It is hard for me to ask someone for a favor.

_____18. I hate it when people offer me sympathy.

_____19. I easily get discouraged when I don't get what I need from others.

_____20. In an argument, I give in easily.

_____21. I don't need much from people.

_____22. I must have one person who is very special to me.

_____23. When I go to a party, I expect that the other people will like me.

_____24. I feel better when I know someone else is in command.

_____25. When I am sick, I prefer that my friends leave me alone.

_____26. I'm never happier than when people say that I have done a good job.

_____27. It is hard for me to make up my mind about a TV show or movie until I know what other people think.

_____28. I am willing to disregard other people's feelings in order to accomplish something that's important to me.

_____29. I need to have one person who puts me above all others.

_____30. In social situations I tend to be very self-conscious.

_____31. I don't need anyone.

_____32. I have a lot of trouble making decisions by myself.

_____33. I tend to imagine the worst if a loved one doesn't arrive when expected.

_____34. Even when things go wrong I can get along without asking for help from my friends.

_____35. I tend to expect too much from others.

_____36. I don't like to buy clothes for myself.

_____37. I tend to be a loner.

_____38. I feel that I never really get all that I need from people.

_____39. When I meet new people, I'm afraid that I won't do the right thing.

_____40. Even if most people turned against me, I could still go on if someone I love stood by me.

_____41. I would rather stay free of involvements with others than to risk disappointments.

_____42. What people think of me doesn't affect how I feel.

_____43. I think that most people don't realize how easily they can hurt me.

_____44. I am very confident about my own judgment.

_____45. I have always had a terrible fear that I will lose the love and support of people I desperately need.

_____46. I don't have what it takes to be a good leader.

_____47. I would feel helpless if deserted by someone I love.

_____48. What other people say doesn't bother me.

SOURCE: Robert M. A. Hirschfeld, Gerald L. Klerman, Harrison G. Gough, James Barrett, Sheldon J. Korchin, and Paul Chodoff. "A measure of interpersonal dependency." _Journal of Personality Assessment,_ 1977, 611–618. Used by permission.

SCORING KEY

There are three subscales on this inventory: Emotional Reliance on Another Person, Lack of Social Self-Confidence, and Autonomy. Add your scores for each group of items.

EMOTIONAL RELIANCE ON ANOTHER PERSON

3, 6, 7, 9, 12, 15, 16, 19, 22, 26, 29, 33, 35, 38, 40, 43, 45, 47

LACK OF SOCIAL SELF-CONFIDENCE

2, 5, 10, *13, 17, 20, 23, *24, 27, 30, 32, 36, 39, 41, 44, *46
(For items marked with an *, score by subtracting your response from 5.)

AUTONOMY

1, 4, 8, 11, 14, 18, 21, 25, 28, 31, 34, 37, 42, 48

HOW DO YOU COMPARE?

	SCORE	PERCENTILE
Emotional Reliance on	30	15
Another Person	35	30
	40	50
	45	70
	50	85
Lack of Social Self-	22	15
Confidence	25	30
	29	50
	33	70
	36	85
Autonomy	21	15
	24	30
	28	50
	32	70
	35	85

About Dependency

Dependency can be a tricky issue. On the one hand, mental health professionals tell us that well-adjusted people form attachments to other people. This process begins when we are infants and we "bond" with our parents. If this bonding is successful, then we will have the capacity to form close, intimate relationships with others as adults. So, we are informed, healthy people allow themselves to be vulnerable. They trust others enough to depend on them. It would seem, then, that dependency is a good thing. Society could not function if we did not have the sense that we could count on others and that they could count on us.

But other experts warn about the dangers of dependency. Dependent people are often described as needy and cloying. And, horror of horrors, they may even be codependent. This point of view suggests that men and women must be strong, independent and autonomous if they are going to make it through life in a satisfying and healthy way.

So, where is the truth? As is so often the case, somewhere in the middle. I believe that people can have a wide range of scores on the subscales of this personality inventory and still be able to function in a perfectly healthy way. Problems are likely to arise only when the scores are either extremely high or extremely low. People can be very concerned about having others in their lives they can count on and still have satisfying relationships. It is only when they feel immobilized when they experience disapproval or when they feel they do not have someone stronger to help them get through life that problems will ensue. On the other hand, people can be very autonomous and free from concern as to what others think of them and still have effective, satisfying lives. It is only when their need for autonomy becomes so strong that they are incapable of forming close relationships with anyone that they are likely to experience distress. If your scores were between the 15th and 85th percentile, it is unlikely that your level of dependency, or autonomy, is an issue that you need concern yourself with.

The authors of the scale provide some empirical evidence to support this contention. In the process of developing their personality inventory, they collected data from both average adults and psychiatric patients. They found that there was not a meaningful difference in the average scores for the two groups on the Emotional Reliance on Another Person subscale and the Autonomy subscale. While dependency issues are often important in psychiatric patients, having strong dependency needs certainly does not mean that one is destined to become a psychiatric patient.

As is the case with a majority of the scales in this book, you might find it instructive to compare your score on this inventory with your partner's—or better yet, a potential partner's. While so much of behavioral research leaves lots of room for interpretation, one thing we psychologists can say with a high degree of certainty is that couples who have similar personality styles are likely to have a more satisfying relationship than couples who are quite different.

Bill and Kelli, a couple I once saw in therapy, illustrate the difficulties that can result from different levels of dependency. Bill was below average in dependency while his wife, Kelli, scored at about the seventieth percentile on the Interpersonal Dependency Inventory. This difference caused the couple a number of misunderstandings and hurt feelings over the years. As just one example, when Bill was sick, he could not stand to be fussed over. He liked to be left completely alone when he wasn't feeling well. The only company he wanted was someone to bring him food and drink. Kelli, on the other hand, loved to be fussed over when she was not feeling well. Her preference was for her husband to sit by her side, uttering sympathetic comments, and leaving only long enough to bring her something from the kitchen. During the early years of their marriage, Kelli believed that Bill's wanting to be left alone was a sign that he was rejecting her. Also, his lack of diligence as a nurse when she was ill was viewed as his not caring about her. Their pattern, repeated many times over the years, was for Kelli to cry about Bill's lack of caring which in turn would inspire Bill to become angry at Kelli's "demanding ways."

Bill and Kelli have been married for more than twenty-five years so they have come to understand each other well, but they have had their rough spots over the years. It is important to remember that differences in dependency levels are common and they do not necessarily reflect how much one person cares about the other.

An autonomous person may be perfectly content with a relationship even though he or she spends lots of time in solitary activities. A dependent partner can't understand how such a person could be so selfish and uncaring. But the reality is that both patterns are preferences, and one is not inherently superior to the other. Life together will be easiest for people who are similar to each other in their level of dependency, but when differences do occur, it is important not to interpret them as reflecting how much one cares about the relationship.

How Competitive Are You?

✓
THE COMPETITIVE-COOPERATIVE ATTITUDE SCALE

DIRECTIONS: For the following statements, indicate the degree to which they describe you or the extent to which you agree using the guidelines below:

5 = Very much like me or strongly agree
4 = Somewhat like me or somewhat agree
3 = Neither like me nor unlike me or neither agree nor disagree
2 = Somewhat unlike me or somewhat disagree
1 = Very much unlike me or strongly disagree

_____ 1. People who get in my way end up paying for it.

_____ 2. The best way to get someone to do something is to use force.

_____ 3. It is all right to do something to someone to get even.

_____ 4. I don't trust very many people.

_____ 5. It is important to treat everyone with kindness.

_____ 6. It doesn't matter whom you hurt on the road to success.

_____ 7. Teamwork is really more important than who wins.

_____ 8. I want to be successful, even if it's at the expense of others.

_____ 9. Do not give anyone a second chance.

_____10. I play a game like my life depended on it.

_____11. I play harder than my teammates.

_____12. All is fair in love and war.

_____13. Nice guys finish last.

_____14. Losers are inferior.

_____15. A group slows me down.

_____16. People need to learn to get along with others as equals.

_____17. My way of doing things is best.

_____18. Every man for himself is the best policy.

_____19. I will do anything to win.

_____20. Winning is the most important part of the game.

_____21. Our country should try harder to achieve peace among all.

_____22. I like to help others.

_____23. Your loss is my gain.

_____24. People who overcome all competitors on the road to success are models for all young people to admire.

_____25. The more I win, the more powerful I feel.

_____26. I like to see the whole class do well on a test.

_____27. I try not to speak unkindly of others.

_____28. I don't like to use pressure to get my way.

SOURCE: Harry J. Martin. "The competitive-cooperative attitude scale." *Psychological Reports,* 1976, 303–306. Used by permission.

SCORING KEY

The items below are reverse scored, so subtract the number you used for these items from 6. After you have done this, simply add up all your numbers for your Competitiveness score.

5	22
7	26
16	27
21	28

HOW DO YOU COMPARE?*

SCORE		PERCENTILE
Men	Women	
53	46	15
60	54	30
68	63	50
76	72	70
83	80	85

*The author of this scale did not include information about norms. The norms provided here are based on a sample of undergraduate students at Old Dominion University. I would like to express my appreciation to Denise Lamm for calculating the statistics upon which these norms are based.

In contrast to your competitiveness score, if you would like to determine how cooperative you are, simply reverse the percentile ranks. So, for example, a man with a score of 53 and a woman with a score of 46 would be at the 85th percentile in "cooperativeness."

About Competitiveness

Is it better to be competitive or cooperative? If there ever was a question where the answer depended on whom you ask, this would be it. I've never met an extremely competitive person who wished he or she could learn to cooperate more, nor have I met an exceptionally cooperative person who wished he or she could develop a competitive edge. Perhaps there are such people in the world, but they must be rare indeed.

My score on this inventory falls close to the fiftieth percentile, so you can guess what my answer to the question will be—there is something to be said for both cooperation and competitiveness. But I will go a step further, which may convince you that I am not taking the position that my personality represents the ideal. I do believe that there are strengths associated with extreme scores at either end of this scale, and I believe that it may be better to have an extreme score—in either direction—than to be like me and score right in the middle. Let me tell you why.

It seems to me that most extremely successful entrepreneurs are highly competitive people. I once read a newspaper article about Bill Gates, the founder of Microsoft, who has become one of the richest men in the world. The article provided examples of tactics used by Microsoft to undermine its competition. I also remember an interview with one of Gates's competitors, who was asked if negotiating with Microsoft was like a street brawl. The competitor answered that it was more like a knife fight. Bill Gates did not come to dominate the computer software market by showing any mercy to his competitors.

On the other hand, I have no doubt that many of Gates's most effective managers would have extreme scores on the cooperation end of the continuum. Complex projects, such as developing a new version of a computer program, require the cooperative effort of hundreds of people, and managers could not possibly accomplish their goals unless they inspired a spirit of teamwork and cooperation. Indeed, research by organizational psychologists does demonstrate that effective leaders tend to value cooperativeness over competitiveness. But keep in mind, these are the people who get the work done, not necessarily the ones who drive their companies to a position of preeminence.

It seems to me there is clearly a place for both competitors and cooperators. If you want to start a new company or if you want to succeed in a sales career, your odds of making it big are probably better if you scored high in competitiveness. On the other hand, if you envision a career as a manager in an established company, you may do better if you place a high value on cooperation.

In a world like ours, people who score somewhere near the middle, as I do, may be at something of a disadvantage. I have had a modestly successful career in academia, but I am nowhere near the top tier of college professors who are widely known for their research programs or their ability to attract grant support. My impression of those who are in that rarefied atmosphere is that, like Gates and his top managers, they fall at one or the other extreme of the cooperation-competition dimension.

Some of these men and women are extremely competitive. They seem driven to publish more articles, to win more grant money, and to achieve more recognition than their colleagues. They cannot accomplish what they do without the help of others, but the people they work with are clearly following orders.

On the other hand, some professors achieve their stature by organizing cooperative research efforts. These people seem to prefer to work in groups of equals. They have the ability to organize large scale projects requiring the efforts of many people, all of whom make a valued contribution.

People like me are not competitive enough to lead an ambitious number of research projects, nor do we enjoy cooperative efforts sufficiently to become part of a productive team. I'm happy enough with the career I've had, but there are times when I wonder what I might have accomplished had I been either more competitive or better at cooperative efforts. I doubt if it is possible to change one's style much when it comes to this personality dimension, but it can be helpful to recognize one's strengths and weaknesses.

One last thought is that I suspect this trait operates somewhat differently in our social relationships than it does in vocational settings. While being either competitive or cooperative may be an advantage in one's career, it may be best to be middle-of-the-road in our social relationships. My friends, for instance, are all competitive enough that it means something to them when they beat me at golf—which happens more than I would like. I would not enjoy playing with someone who did not care if he won or lost. But there are a few people I avoid playing with because they are so competitive that they can be obnoxious and even abusive in a close match. A touch of competitiveness can add texture to friendships, but these relationships require a healthy dose of cooperative spirit if they are to thrive.

Are You an Argumentative Person?

✓

THE ARGUMENTATIVENESS SCALE

DIRECTIONS: This questionnaire contains statements about arguing controversial issues. Indicate how often each statement is true for you personally by placing the appropriate number in the blank to the left of the statement.

> 1 = Almost never true
> 2 = Rarely true
> 3 = Occasionally true
> 4 = Often true
> 5 = Almost always true

_____ 1. While in an argument, I worry that the person I am arguing with will form a negative impression of me.

_____ 2. Arguing over controversial issues improves my intelligence.

_____ 3. I enjoy avoiding arguments.

_____ 4. I am energetic and enthusiastic when I argue.

_____ 5. Once I finish an argument I promise myself that I will not get into another.

_____ 6. Arguing with a person creates more problems than it solves.

_____ 7. I have a pleasant, good feeling when I win a point in an argument.

_____ 8. When I finish arguing with someone, I feel nervous and upset.

_____ 9. I enjoy a good argument over a controversial issue.

_____10. I get an unpleasant feeling when I realize I am about to get into an argument.

_____11. I enjoy defending my point of view on an issue.

_____12. I am happy when I keep an argument from happening.

_____13. I do not like to miss the opportunity to argue a controversial issue.

_____14. I prefer being with people who rarely disagree with me.

_____15. I consider an argument an exciting intellectual challenge.

_____16. I find myself unable to think of effective points during an argument.

_____17. I feel refreshed and satisfied after an argument on a controversial issue.

_____18. I have the ability to do well in an argument.

_____19. I try to avoid getting into arguments.

_____20. I feel excitement when I expect that a conversation I am in is leading to an argument.

SOURCE: Dominic A. Infante and A. S. Rancer. "A conceptualization and measure of argumentativeness." *Journal of Personality Assessment,* 1982, 72–80. Used by permission.

SCORING KEY FOR THE
ARGUMENTATIVENESS SCALE

Add up the numbers that you have recorded for items 1, 3, 5, 6, 8, 10, 12, 14, 16, and 19. This score reflects your tendency to avoid getting into arguments. Next, add up the numbers that you have recorded for items 2, 4, 7, 9, 11, 13, 15, 17, 18, and 20. This score indicates your tendency to seek out arguments. To obtain a total score, subtract the first score, your tendency to avoid arguments, from the second score. The norms below will provide you with an idea as to how you compare with others.

HOW DO YOU COMPARE?

SCORE	PERCENTILE
−7	15
−1	30
4	50
9	70
15	85

About Argumentativeness

This is one scale where it is better to score close to the 50th percentile than it is to have a score at either extreme. People with high scores like nothing better than a good argument; they live for it. For these people, it is a form of entertainment that beats going to a movie every time. Low scorers will go to great lengths to avoid arguments. They view them as a form of conflict and hostility that can only drive a wedge between people. They want everyone to be nice and to get along. Both of these styles can cause problems.

Let's take a look first at those who love to argue. The problem with having an affinity for a good argument is that it can so easily be overdone. I have a good friend—I'll call him Ted—who is a chronic arguer (he's never read a self-help book in his life, so I know I'm safe). When I'm with him, I know that if I express most any opinion it will lead to more than a simple exchange of views. As an example, one day while we were playing golf I stated that I thought Phil Michelson, who had just turned pro after winning a tour event as an amateur, would eventually join the ranks of the truly great golfers. Ted immediately disagreed. He gave me a ten-minute lecture about all the gifted amateurs who had disappointing pro careers. He tried to pin me down about how many tournaments I thought Michelson would win, and I finally ended the discussion by agreeing to a $10 bet that he would win eight major tournaments by the year 2013. But I was naive to think that would put an end to it. We then had to discuss whether we were betting a flat $10 or whether it would be adjusted to reflect inflation. And finally we had to talk about what index we would use to make the adjustment. I really do enjoy Ted's company, but there are times when he just wears me out.

One thing that Ted is very good about (and the reason he is still my friend) that other arguers are not—he sticks to the issue. He never makes his arguments personal. He has never accused me of being incapable of understanding the topic under discussion or of being ill-informed. He shows respect for my opinions even though he makes it clear he thinks they are wrong. Unlike Ted, many arguers mistake their aggressiveness and hostility for assertiveness. They believe that anything said during the heat of the argument is fair, no matter how much it hurts the other person. Their goal is to win their point, and if it takes a personal attack to do it, so be it.

If you scored at the 85th percentile or above, think about the kind of arguer you are. If you say disparaging things about your opponent, if your favorite cliche is "all's fair in love and war," you may be winning your points, but you are surely losing friends. You are a bully, and you should cut it out.

If you are more like Ted, all you have to do is tone it down a little. Stop when you have made all your points, even if your opponent remains unconvinced. Discussions do not have to have winners and losers; they only require participants. Most everyone likes to exchange views and opinions, but it does not always have to turn into a contest of intellect and will. And if you are like Ted, you may not even realize what you are doing. Ted has been surprised when his desire to turn every discussion into an argument has been pointed out to him. He hasn't changed, but at least he can view his tendencies with good humor—and indeed, that's good enough for me and his other friends.

If you scored at the 15th percentile or lower, you too confuse assertiveness and aggressiveness, only you tend to view any act of assertion as aggressive and hostile. Assertiveness and aggressiveness are two very different qualities. Assertiveness means expressing your opinion in a socially acceptable fashion. It does not mean saying nasty things to other people during the heat of a discussion, nor does it mean that you must persist until your opponent capitulates.

Extremely low scorers on this scale are viewed as nice guys. And they are—they wouldn't dream of hurting anyone's feelings. But they are also viewed as being somewhat bland and uninteresting. It is hard to feel like you know someone who never expresses an opinion for fear that it will turn into an argument. If this describes you, you may want to make an effort to speak up more. Remember, most everyone enjoys a good discussion, and that requires you to express your thoughts and opinions.

You don't even have to tell others they are wrong in order to have a good discussion. Concentrate on "I" statements. Say things such as "I've always thought . . ." or "It seems to me . . ." As long as you never tell others explicitly that they are stupid or misinformed, they will not resent you for your views. And they will probably appreciate getting a clearer idea of the kind of person you are.

SECTION IV

GETTING TOGETHER

This section will provide you with information about whether you have the qualities it takes to have successful romantic relationships. After you complete the tests in this section, you will know—

A. How you love your partner.
B. How capable you are of having an intimate relationship.
C. How romantic you are.
D. How jealous you are.
E. How positively you feel toward your partner.

How Do You Love Your Partner?

THE TRIANGULAR LOVE SCALE

DIRECTIONS: To complete the following scale, fill in the blank spaces with the name of one person you love or care about deeply. Then rate your agreement with each of the items by using a nine-point scale in which 1 = "not at all," 5 = "moderately," and 9 = "extremely." Use points in between to indicate intermediate levels of agreement between these values.

_____ 1. I am actively supportive of _____'s well-being.

_____ 2. I have a warm relationship with _____.

_____ 3. I am able to count on _____ in times of need.

_____ 4. _____ is able to count on me in times of need.

_____ 5. I am willing to share myself and my possessions with _____.

_____ 6. I receive considerable emotional support from _____.

_____ 7. I give considerable emotional support to _____.

_____ 8. I communicate well with _____.

_____ 9. I value _____ greatly in my life.

_____10. I feel close to _____.

_____ 11. I have a comfortable relationship with _____.

_____ 12. I feel that I really understand _____.

_____ 13. I feel that _____ really understands me.

_____ 14. I feel that I can really trust _____.

_____ 15. I share deeply personal information about myself with _____.

_____ 16. Just seeing _____ excites me.

_____ 17. I find myself thinking about _____ frequently during the day.

_____ 18. My relationship with _____ is very romantic.

_____ 19. I find _____ to be very personally attractive.

_____ 20. I idealize _____.

_____ 21. I cannot imagine another person making me as happy as _____ does.

_____ 22. I would rather be with _____ than with anyone else.

_____ 23. There is nothing more important to me than my relationship with _____.

_____ 24. I especially like physical contact with _____.

_____ 25. There is something almost "magical" about my relationship with _____.

_____ 26. I adore _____.

_____ 27. I cannot imagine life without _____.

_____ 28. My relationship with _____ is passionate.

_____ 29. When I see romantic movies and read romantic books I think of _____.

_____30. I fantasize about _____.

_____31. I know that I care about _____.

_____32. I am committed to maintaining my relationship with _____.

_____33. Because of my commitment to _____, I would not let other people come between us.

_____34. I have confidence in the stability of my relationship with _____.

_____35. I could not let anything get in the way of my commitment to _____.

_____36. I expect my love for _____ to last for the rest of my life.

_____37. I will always feel a strong responsibility for _____.

_____38. I view my commitment to _____ as a solid one.

_____39. I cannot imagine ending my relationship with _____.

_____40. I am certain of my love for _____.

_____41. I view my relationship with _____ as permanent.

_____42. I view my relationship with _____ as a good decision.

_____43. I feel a sense of responsibility toward _____.

_____44. I plan to continue my relationship with _____.

_____45. Even when _____ is hard to deal with, I remain committed to our relationship.

SOURCE: "The Triangular Love Scale" from *The Triangle of Love: Intimacy, Passion, Commitment,* by Robert Sternberg. Copyright © 1988 by Basic Books, Inc. Reprinted by permission of BasicBooks, a division of Harper-Collins Publishers, Inc.

SCORING KEY FOR STERNBERG'S
TRIANGULAR LOVE SCALE

Robert Sternberg's scale reflects his conclusion that there are three components to love—passion, intimacy, and commitment—so you will need to find three separate scores for this scale. The first 15 items reflect intimacy, the second 15 measure passion, and the final 15 items reflect commitment. Add your scores for each group of 15 items to find the degree to which you experience these three components of love for your partner. You can use the information below to see how you stand with respect to a comparison group of men and women, with an average age of 31, who were either married or in a close relationship.

HOW DO YOU COMPARE?

	Score		Percentile
Intimacy	Passion	Commitment	
93	73	85	15
102	85	96	30
111	98	108	50
120	110	120	70
129	123	131	85

About Love

Sternberg says that love is like a triangle and the best kind of love is an equilateral triangle—one in which all three sides are of equal length. What he means, of course, is that there are three components to love—intimacy, passion, and commitment—and that love is best when we experience all three of these emotions and in approximately equal intensities. So you are fortunate indeed if your scores on all three subscales were above average and about the same.

If your scores on the three dimensions of love were widely different or if you had one or two scores below average, it does not necessarily mean that your relationship is in trouble. All relationships have their ups and downs, and it is likely to be the case that the scores you would obtain a year from now might be quite different from the scores you had today. You might want to take the test a second time and respond as you would when you are feeling best about your partner. This could give you an indication of the potential of your relationship.

Your scores are also likely to reflect how long you have been with your partner. We tend to become involved in a romantic relationship because we experience the right "chemistry"—or what Sternberg calls passion. So this component is usually highest during the first year or two of a relationship. While passion tends to lose its intensity over time, the most successful relationships continue to maintain a healthy dose of this element.

The second stage of a relationship is generally marked by the development of intimacy. Once we decide we are attracted to and interested in a person, we begin to confide in him or her, we want to share all our secrets with this person, to tell our loved one our life story. This component tends to reach its peak a year or two after the relationship has begun, but the most successful relationships maintain a high level of intimacy indefinitely.

At some point—maybe after six months, maybe six years—we develop a sense of commitment for our partner. We value the relationship enough that we will do whatever we can to maintain it. It is this sense of commitment that helps us weather the difficult times that are a part of every relationship. Commitment tends to be strongest for couples who have been together for several years.

The happiest couples are those who have similar love triangles for each other. Sternberg, who obviously remembers his high school geometry well, calls this congruency. In other words, if you have strong passion for your partner but are a little low on intimacy, you are likely to have problems if your partner is highest on intimacy and lowest on passion. We are happiest in a relationship when our partner feels about us the way we would like him or her to. You may want your partner to complete this test so you can determine how compatible the two of you are. It would be nice to discover that the two of you have congruent love triangles.

"How do I love thee? Let me count the ways." Sternberg's answer would be that there are eight possible ways. He arrives at this number by looking at the possible combinations of his three components of love. By judging the relative strength of your three components, you can use the information below to determine how you love your partner.

Nonlove None of the three components of love are present in this type of relationship. This is the type of relationship we have with most people we interact with on a day-to-day basis. If this describes your feelings for your partner or your partner's feelings for you, your relationship is on shaky ground.

Liking This is the feeling we have when passion and commitment are weak or absent but intimacy is high. This is most likely to describe our feelings for our close friends.

Infatuation This is what often motivates us to develop a relationship. Infatuation is used to describe those relationships where passion is high but intimacy and commitment are low.

Empty Love This exists when commitment is high but passion and intimacy are low or absent. It is most likely to be found in couples who have been married for years, perhaps for the sake of the children, and want to maintain their relationship even though they share neither their minds nor their bodies.

Romantic Love Romantic love is most common in couples whose relationship is relatively new. Their passion and intimacy are high, but they have not been together long enough or shared enough experiences to develop a strong sense of commitment to each other.

Companionate Love Intimacy and commitment are strong in this type of love but passion is low. It is most often found in couples who have been together for some time and are happy with each other, but their sexual attraction has faded.

Fatuous Love Passion and commitment are high while intimacy is low in this type of love. It describes couples who experience a powerful chemistry and decide to marry on that basis even though they may not know each other very well. Sometimes these couples develop a sense of intimacy after they have made the commitment. Sometimes they learn they do not really like each other very much.

Consummate Love The ideal type of love, in which all three components are strong; the type of love we all hope and strive for. As Sternberg suggests, this state may be easier to achieve than to maintain.

May you and your partner find consummate love.

How Capable Are You of Being Intimate?

✓

> **INTIMACY ATTITUDE SCALE—REVISED**

DIRECTIONS: The following items reflect feelings and attitudes that people have toward others and relationships with others. Specifically the items are concerned with attitudes of closeness, intimacy, and trust. Fill in each space with the letter that most closely describes your feelings about the item.

> A. Strongly disagree
> B. Mildly disagree
> C. Agree and disagree equally
> D. Mildly agree
> E. Strongly agree

_____ 1. I like to share my feelings with others.

_____ 2. I like to feel close to other people.

_____ 3. I like to listen to other people talk about their feelings.

_____ 4. I am concerned with rejection in my expression of feelings to others.

158

_____ 5. I'm concerned with being dominated in a close relationship with another.

_____ 6. I'm often anxious about my own acceptance in a close relationship.

_____ 7. I'm concerned that I trust other people too much.

_____ 8. Expression of emotion makes me feel close to another person.

_____ 9. I do not want to express feelings that would hurt another person.

_____10. I am overly critical of people in a close relationship.

_____11. I want to feel close to people to whom I am attracted.

_____12. I tend to reveal my deepest feelings to other people.

_____13. I'm afraid to talk about my sexual feelings with a person to whom I'm very interested.

_____14. I want to be close to a person who is attracted to me.

_____15. I would not become too close because it involves conflict.

_____16. I seek out close relationships with people to whom I am attracted.

_____17. When people become close they tend not to listen to each other.

_____18. Intimate relationships bring me great satisfaction.

_____19. I search for close intimate relationships.

_____20. It is important to me to form close relationships.

_____21. I do not need to share my feelings and thoughts with others.

_____22. When I become very close to another, I am likely to see things that are hard for me to accept.

_____23. I tend to accept most things about people with whom I share a close relationship.

_____24. I defend my personal space so others do not come too close.

_____25. I tend to distrust people who are concerned with closeness and intimacy.

_____26. I have concerns about losing my individuality in close relationships.

_____27. I have concerns about giving up control if I enter into a really intimate relationship.

_____28. Being honest and open with another person makes me feel closer to that person.

_____29. If I were another person, I would be interested in getting to know me.

_____30. I only become close to people with whom I share common interests.

_____31. Revealing secrets about my sex life makes me feel close to others.

_____32. Generally, I can feel just as close to someone of the same sex as someone of the other sex.

_____33. When another person is physically attracted to me, I usually want to become more intimate.

_____ 34. I have difficulty being intimate with more than one person.

_____ 35. Being open and intimate with another person usually makes me feel good.

_____ 36. I usually can see another person's point of view.

_____ 37. I want to be sure that I am in good control of myself before I attempt to become intimate with another person.

_____ 38. I resist intimacy.

_____ 39. Stories of interpersonal relationships tend to affect me.

_____ 40. Undressing with members of a group increases my feelings of intimacy.

_____ 41. I try to trust and be close to others.

_____ 42. I think that people who want to become intimate have hidden reasons for wanting closeness.

_____ 43. When I become intimate with another person, the possibility of my being manipulated is increased.

_____ 44. I am generally a secretive person.

_____ 45. I feel that sex and intimacy are the same, and one cannot exist without the other.

_____ 46. I can only be intimate in a physical relationship.

_____ 47. The demands placed on me by those with whom I have intimate relationships often inhibit my own satisfaction.

_____ 48. I would compromise to maintain an intimate relationship.

_____49. When I am physically attracted to another, I usually want to become intimate with the person.

_____50. I understand and accept that intimacy leads to bad feelings as well as good feelings.

SOURCE: Edmund Amidon, V. K. Kumar, and Thomas Treadwell. "Measurement of Intimacy Attitudes: The Intimacy Attitude Scale—Revised." *Journal of Personality Assessment,* 1983, 635–639. Used by permission.

SCORING KEY FOR THE IAS—R

For the items below, use the following scoring key:

$$A = 1 \text{ point}$$
$$B = 2 \text{ points}$$
$$C = 3 \text{ points}$$
$$D = 4 \text{ points}$$
$$E = 5 \text{ points}$$

1	14	28	36
2	16	29	39
3	18	31	41
8	19	32	48
11	20	33	49
12	23	35	50

The items on the following page are reverse scored. For these items, use the following scale.

$$A = 5 \text{ points}$$
$$B = 4 \text{ points}$$
$$C = 3 \text{ points}$$
$$D = 2 \text{ points}$$
$$E = 1 \text{ point}$$

4	13	25	38	46
5	15	26	40	47
6	17	27	42	
7	21	30	43	
9	22	34	44	
10	24	37	45	

Add your totals for the two groups of items to obtain your final score. The higher your score, the greater your capacity and desire for intimate relationships.

HOW DO YOU COMPARE?

SCORE	PERCENTILE
150	15
161	30
172	50
183	70
194	85

About Intimacy

Probably every expert would agree that the ability to have intimate relationships is a highly desirable quality. And indeed, Dr. Thomas Treadwell and his colleague, who constructed the Intimacy Attitude Scale—Revised, presented evidence to suggest that high scores on their scale are related to a variety of other desirable qualities. They reported that people with high scores on their scale tended to engage in more intimate behaviors, they tended to self-disclose more to others, they tended to feel in control of their fate, they tended to be more active, and they tended to experience less alienation from friends, family, and self. This would seem to be good evidence for what the authors of countless self-help books have been saying for years—that if we are to have happy, satisfying lives, we must develop the ability to have intimate relationships with others.

I may be among the minority of psychologists on this point, but I believe that the emphasis on intimacy has been overdone. I would agree that those who are invariably leery of others, who believe that sharing any feelings with anyone is a sign of weakness, are destined to be lonely, unhappy people. But I also believe that those individuals who are on a perpetual quest to find intimacy can be extremely tiresome. For those of you who are old enough to remember the encounter-group movement of the 1970s, you undoubtedly can recall how insufferable your friends could be the first few weeks after they completed their sensitivity training. I know I was after my encounter-group experience, but thankfully, it wore off rather quickly. All that indiscriminate openness and honesty was a downright pain.

Like so many aspects of life, when it comes to intimacy, moderation is the key. People should pick their spots carefully. Certainly, it is desirable to have a high level of intimacy with a spouse or long-term partner. The most valuable aspect of such relationships, it seems to me, is to know that you have a best friend who will always be in your corner; someone with whom you can share your fears and doubts and who can be counted on to provide the extra support when it's needed.

But even with a partner, it is possible to overdo the quest for intimacy. While most of us would feel close to someone who shared his or her deepest, darkest secrets, we don't want to hear about them every day. I've seen a number of couples who split up because one partner could not stop burdening the other with self-doubts and fears. There comes a point, which is different for everyone and every couple, when a person has to say, "Enough. I've listened to what's on your mind, and now it's time to move on to other things."

Most people are happier if they have a few close friends they can be intimate with. But again, selectivity is important. It is not necessary to share every thought with every friend. While it is difficult to feel close to someone who rarely shares any personal details of his or her life, it is possible to share too much. It has never happened to me, but my wife Meredith has cooled friendships because they became too intense. Meredith had a high score on the Intimacy scale, but she has had a few friends who drained her. She said that spending time with them began to feel like therapy rather than friendship. She likes to feel helpful when her friends are having problems, but she wants to have a little fun too.

Like most of the tests in this book, this one was constructed to help researchers learn more about intimacy and not as a tool to be used in making clinical assessments. Consequently, if you received a very low score or a very high score, it does not necessarily mean that you are abnormal. The statistics were based on a group of average people, and no attempt was made to include those who were having problems related to their attitudes toward intimacy. If you did receive an extreme score, however, it may mean that you could profit from taking a close look at yourself. If your score was 140 or lower, you might ask yourself if you close yourself off from others more than necessary. If you feel lonely or isolated, your low score might provide an explanation of why you feel this way. If your score was 210 or higher, you may want to examine whether you might be overwhelming the people in your life with your intensity. Perhaps if you backed off just a bit, people would enjoy your company more.

Perhaps the most important thing to look at is whether you and your partner have similar scores. I believe that two reserved people can have just as happy and satisfying a relationship as two people who share every last thought, but you can experience a great deal of frustration if your partner's score is considerably different from your own. There is no scientific basis for stating just how large this difference can be before it is likely to cause problems, but I would guess that if two people's scores differ by 40 points or more, they could be in for some difficult times. If you fall into this category, talk about it with your partner. Discuss your reactions to the individual items. The more you know about your partner, the sounder your basis for having a successful relationship.

Dr. Treadwell did not provide separate statistics for men and women, but it is likely that men, on the average, will have somewhat lower scores than women. It also seems likely, based on psychological research, that men will interpret many of the items differently than women. As just one example, take a look at the first item, "I like to share my feelings with others." A man may respond "Agree" because he likes to talk about his golf scores or his business successes with his friends. His wife might also select "Agree," thinking that she likes to talk with her friends about the problems she is having with her parents or her feelings about her teenaged daughter's boyfriend. Simply put, men and women can have very different ideas about what it means to be intimate.

How Romantic Are You?

✓

THE ROMANTICISM SCALE

DIRECTIONS: Below are statements obtained from young people in love and from magazine articles, newspaper articles, and books about love. For this quiz, give your opinion about each item. There are no right or wrong answers.

For each of the items below, use the following key:

> 1 = Strongly disagree
> 2 = Mildly disagree
> 3 = Agree and disagree equally
> 4 = Mildly agree
> 5 = Strongly agree

_____ 1. Love is that strange feeling that overtakes one person on account of another person.

_____ 2. One can't help falling in love if he/she meets the right person.

_____ 3. "Every time we are near each other, we get a funny feeling inside" is a good sign of love.

_____ 4. One doesn't "fall in love," it has to be achieved.

_____ 5. The wish to be with someone constantly is a good sign of love.

_____ 6. Perfect love means one is always satisfied with one's partner.

_____ 7. Marriage for convenience can be successful.

_____ 8. One can experience true love only once.

_____ 9. True love is not based at all on physical attraction.

_____10. People in love are often oblivious to their surroundings.

_____11. Problems always work out when two people are really in love.

_____12. Love usually makes the heart beat faster.

_____13. The strength of your feelings toward each other demonstrates the fact that you were made for each other.

_____14. Love can develop after marriage.

_____15. People do not need to have a long engagement if they are meant for each other.

_____16. True love lasts forever.

_____17. Love sometimes gives one a sick feeling.

_____18. When in love, it is hard to see the other's faults.

_____19. A loss of appetite usually accompanies true love.

_____20. Love is an all-or-nothing feeling; there is no in-between.

_____21. When in love, one should just love and not reason why.

_____22. One in love will never be bored.

_____23. One shouldn't strive to maintain love.

_____24. Marriage requires hard work in order to succeed.

_____25. Love will find a way.

_____26. If it's true love, one won't need to actively seek the other.

_____27. Happiness is inevitable in true love.

_____28. Love doesn't happen; it's learned.

_____29. People in love are always considerate.

_____30. It's love if it makes you feel good.

_____31. You really fall in love just once in a lifetime.

SOURCE: This scale is a modified form of the "Dean's Romanticism Scale," constructed by the late Dr. Dwight G. Dean. Dr. Dean presented this scale in a paper read at The Groves Conference on Marriage and the Family, The Ohio State University, Columbus, Ohio, April 4, 1960.

SCORING KEY

Find your total score for the following items:

1	11	19	27
2	12	20	29
3	13	21	30
5	15	22	31
6	16	23	
8	17	25	
10	18	26	

The following items are reverse scored. Subtract your response from 6 for each of the items, and after finding your total for these items, add it to the total for the items on the preceding page for your final score.

4	18
7	24
9	28
14	

HOW DO YOU COMPARE?

SCORE	PERCENTILE
75	15
80	30
86	50
92	70
97	85

About Romanticism

Morton Hunt, the prolific social science writer, has observed that we Americans are firmly of two minds when it comes to love; we believe in every tenet of romantic love, but we know perfectly well things don't really work that way. I tend to agree with Hunt, but I would expand his thesis to suggest that one's belief about romantic love depends on the state of one's own love life. When we are in love's grasp, we tend to endorse romantic notions such as "Love conquers all." But after we have been in a love relationship for a few years, we heartily endorse the notion that "Love is not enough." Like so many areas of life, experience makes it difficult to remain idealistic about romantic love.

The norms provided here were based upon a sample of college students, who tend to be more romantic than older, more experienced adults. So if you're too old to qualify for Generation X status, even if your score places you below the 15th percentile, you're not necessarily hopelessly cynical. You may simply have the wisdom that sometimes comes with age.

I realize I may sound cynical about romantic love, and perhaps I am. While I do believe there isn't a feeling that even comes close to being as exhilarating as being in love, I also have seen too many couples who based their decision to marry on their intense emotional attachment for each other, only to learn later that they were completely incompatible in every other way. Being in love is a wonderful experience, but it is not sufficient justification for making a decision that will affect the rest of your life. When choosing a lifelong partner, we need to be as objective, rational, and clearheaded as possible. Unfortunately, being in love often makes it difficult to summon these qualities. Several researchers have documented the common observation that we tend to view our lover through rose-colored glasses.

As you may suspect, there are differences between men and women when it comes to romantic love, although the nature of the differences may surprise you. Until recently, men have typically received higher scores than women on scales such as the one presented here. Men were more likely to believe that one should marry for love regardless of differences in background, attitudes, or personality. Women have tended to be more practical, perhaps even calculating—reluctant to marry a man they were in love with if he did not possess other qualities they were looking for.

The explanation for this difference was that, traditionally, a woman's standard of living was largely determined by the man she chose to spend her life with. Men could afford to be romantic. Their choice of a wife was not likely to determine the neighborhood they could live in, the quality of the clothes they could wear, or whether they could afford to send their children to college. Women had good reason to ignore their hearts.

A generation ago, when increasing numbers of women began to pursue their own careers, several social scientists observed that as women started to achieve more financial independence, they might also become more romantic; and this does seem to have happened. Surveys conducted during the past few years have found few, if any, differences between college men and women in how they respond to romanticism scales.

But some differences between the sexes seem to persist. Dr. Zick Rubin, one of the foremost "love researchers," has found that men are more likely than women to want to fall in love, they are less likely to end a relationship, and they suffer more when a relationship ends. Interestingly, even when a relationship is more important to the woman than it is to the man, the woman is more likely to end it if she feels it will not be best for her in the long run. Women still seem to be capable of more objectivity when it comes to love than men.

Let us return, for a moment, to Hunt's observation that we are firmly of two minds when it comes to romantic love. What he meant was that most of us are smart enough and rational enough not to let our hearts rule our lives. We all want to fall in love, but we have the wisdom to fall in love with people who are similar to ourselves in terms of background, temperament, and values—factors that are important to a stable relationship. Even if we pay lip service to notions of romanticism, part of us remains objective enough to make relatively good choices when it comes to selecting a partner.

A very high score on this scale could mean that you cause problems for yourself by allowing your emotions to overcome your reason. For instance, young women who have an unwanted pregnancy have higher romanticism scores than those who do not. A more common problem among the extremely romantic is the tendency to make commitments too quickly, and then to become disillusioned once the feelings of romantic love inevitably begin to fade. I know one woman in her 40s, an otherwise bright and successful individual, who is planning her third divorce after being married this time for less than two years. As Janet describes her situation, "I fell hard for Allen, and I really wanted to have a child with him before I was too old. But after the baby was born, I saw how dull and uninteresting Allen was. As soon as I get my business back on its feet, I'm going to leave him."

Sadly for Janet, she does not have enough insight into her pattern to realize how her romanticism is harming her life. Barbara, on the other hand, has Janet's romantic ideals, but she has learned to keep them in their place. Consider her story: "I married Tim when I was 19 because I was hopelessly in love with him. It didn't take me long to realize that he was a real bum, and I was lucky that I got out as easily as I did. I know I fall in love easily, but I swore I'd never make the same mistake again. When I met Ray, I was deeply in love before a month passed, but I told him that I wouldn't marry him until we lived together for a while. After two years, when my heart no longer pounded when I expected to see him, I knew that I could be objective enough to make the right decision. My rose-colored glasses were in the closet. We did get married, and we're still happy five years later."

Barbara's story may not be the most romantic, but her life is much better than Janet's. Being romantic is nice, I suppose, and being in love is truly wonderful, but most people would be much better off if they could view it as the icing on the cake rather than as the basis for making a commitment to a relationship.

How Jealous Are You?

DIRECTIONS: The following scale list some situations in which you may have been involved, or in which you could be involved. Rate them with regard to how you would feel if you were confronted with the situation by selecting the number that corresponds to one of the reactions shown below.

> 0 = Pleased
> 1 = Mildly upset
> 2 = Upset
> 3 = Very upset
> 4 = Extremely upset

_____ 1. Your partner expresses the desire that you both develop other romantic relationships.

_____ 2. Your partner spends increasingly more time at work with a fellow employee you feel could be sexually attractive to your partner.

_____ 3. Your partner suddenly shows an interest in going to a party when he or she finds out that someone will be there with whom he or she has been romantically involved previously.

174

_____ 4. At a party, your partner hugs someone other than you.

_____ 5. You notice your partner repeatedly looking at another person.

_____ 6. Your partner spends increasingly more time in outside activities and hobbies in which you are not interested.

_____ 7. At a party, your partner kisses someone you do not know.

_____ 8. Your boss, with whom you have had a good working relationship in the past, now seems to be more interested in the work of a coworker.

_____ 9. Your partner goes to a bar several evenings without you.

_____ 10. Your partner recently received a promotion, and the new position requires a great deal of travel, business dinners, and parties, most of which you are not invited to attend.

_____ 11. At a party, your partner dances with someone you do not know.

_____ 12. You and a coworker worked very hard on an extremely important project. However, your boss gave your coworker full credit for it.

_____ 13. Someone flirts with your partner.

_____ 14. At a party, your partner repeatedly kisses someone you do not know.

_____ 15. Your partner has sexual relations with someone else.

_____ 16. Your brother or sister was given more freedom, such as staying up later or driving the car.

_____ 17. Your partner comments to you on how attractive another person is.

_____ 18. While at a social gathering of a group of friends, your partner spends little time talking to you, but engages the others in animated conversation.

_____ 19. Grandparents visit your family, and they seem to devote most of their attention to a brother or sister instead of you.

_____ 20. Your partner flirts with someone else.

_____ 21. Your brother or sister seems to be receiving more affection and/or attention from your parents.

_____ 22. You have just discovered your partner is having an affair with someone at work.

_____ 23. The person who has been your assistant for a number of years at work decides to take a similar position with some other company.

_____ 24. The group to which you belong appears to be leaving you out of plans, activities, etc.

_____ 25. Your best friend suddenly shows interest in doing things with someone else.

SOURCE: Robert G. Bringle, S. Roach, C. Andler, and S. Evenbeck. "Measuring the intensity of jealous reactions." *Catalog of Selected Documents in Psychology,* 1979, *9,* 23–24. Used by permission.

SCORING KEY FOR THE SELF-REPORT JEALOUSY SCALE

Simply add together the numbers you used for each item. The total is your jealousy score.

HOW DO YOU COMPARE?

Score	Percentile
58	15
65	30
71	50
77	70
83	85

About Jealousy

Is there a more frightening and dangerous monster than the one with green eyes? I'm not sure there is. All you have to do is read the newspaper for a few weeks to find several instances where jealousy has been the motive for acts of violence and cruelty. Husbands murder wives. Girlfriends kill boyfriends. Mistresses shoot both wives and husbands. It happens every day. And there are countless other stories that never make the newspapers. Stalking, spouse abuse, kidnapping—so many hurtful acts have their roots in jealousy.

I think what surprises me most about jealousy is how many people see it as a perfectly legitimate and appropriate emotion. I remember watching a television news-magazine show in which a number of high school boys talked about their relationships with their girlfriends. A majority of them agreed it was OK to hit a date if she flirted with another boy at a party. And even more astounding, there were several girls who agreed with this view.

Every semester I ask the students in my Human Sexuality class if they feel that it is inevitable to experience jealousy in a romantic relationship, and a substantial majority of them say it is. Some of them even say that you can measure how much you love someone by how jealous you are. And a significant minority will speak blithely about shooting a partner should he or she be discovered with someone else.

How can this be? Don't people understand how destructive and hurtful jealousy is? Don't they realize that jealousy has never made a relationship better and it has caused any number to end—sometimes violently?

If you had a high score on this scale, it does not necessarily mean that you are such a jealous person that you are prone to violence. The scale is intended to be used with a normal population. But, on the other hand, a high score does mean that your feelings of jealousy are probably causing some problems in your relationships, and you may benefit by taking a close look at yourself.

It is important to distinguish between feelings of insecurity and feelings of jealousy. It probably is inevitable to feel somewhat insecure about a romantic relationship, especially in its early stages. When we first fall in love, we want evidence that our partner cares as much about us as we do about him or her. So if we see our loved one talking animatedly to someone else at a party, we can't help but worry that he or she finds this other person more interesting than us.

But that's not jealousy. Jealousy is an angry, aggressive emotion. It demands that we take action, that we strike out at those who have betrayed us.

People who experience intense feelings of jealousy are

not happy people. First of all, they tend to be low in self-esteem. They do not feel very good about themselves, for they have difficulty believing that anyone else could care deeply about them. Thus, it is not surprising that when they see their partner talking to someone else, their first thoughts are of betrayal. They expect it because deep down they "know" they are not good enough to deserve their partner's loyalty.

Jealous people are nervous people who see the world as a frightening place. They expect the worst of people, including the ones they love. They become hypervigilant in their search for evidence that their worst fears are indeed reality. So a partner's friendly smile to a stranger becomes a sign of a secret affair. Talking too long to a friend on the telephone is taken as evidence of a lack of caring. No, jealousy is not an attractive quality.

If you are a jealous person, all is not lost—you can change. It will take some work, but I am confident that you will find the effort worthwhile. You must convince yourself that it is in your own self-interest to rid yourself of this destructive emotion. Of all the couples I have seen in therapy, I have never seen a case in which jealousy made the relationship better. And I've seen many relationships in which jealousy has destroyed any future the couple might have had. At first, your partner might be flattered by your jealousy. If you are lucky, it might be seen as a sign of how much you care. But before long, your partner will find your questions and accusations suffocating. It will surely drive a wedge between the two of you, and unless you change, the odds are good that you will find yourself alone.

You must talk to yourself. You must tell yourself that your fears are groundless. You must restrain yourself. Don't interrogate your partner when he or she is a half-hour late. Give your partner a big hug and tell her how

glad you are to see him or her. Even if your suspicions
have some basis in reality, you must remind yourself that
angry words won't bring your partner back. You have a
much better chance of winning your partner's loyalty by
reminding him or her of how much you care and that you
would like to talk about any problems the two of you may
be having.

Being a nonjealous person does not mean that you have
to accept anything your partner does. I have never had a
problem with jealousy, but I wouldn't like it if my wife
locked herself in a bedroom with another man at a party.
You have the right to expect that both you and your partner will abide by certain ground rules. If your partner vio-
lates one of these rules, you should bring it to his or her
attention. You might say, "It hurts me and makes me very
uncomfortable when you act like that around our
friends." And depending on the seriousness of the trans-
gression, you can lay out the alternatives. If your partner
flirted shamelessly with an attractive man or woman at a
party, you might tell him or her, "You embarrassed me
tonight, and if you do it again I won't go to another party
with you." If your partner left the party with an attractive
man or woman and didn't return home until the morn-
ing, you might tell him or her, "I can't live with you if you
plan to spend nights with other people. You have to decide if you want me or your freedom."

The point is that you must let your partner know how
you feel and how you view the options. By giving your
partner a choice, you have a chance of getting what you
want. By demanding that your partner comply to your
wishes, especially if your demands are hostile and abusive,
you are guaranteeing that you will lose in the long run.

How Do You Feel About Your Partner?

✓

DIRECTIONS: Below is a list of questions about various feelings between engaged/married people. Using the scale below, answer each one of them in terms of how you *generally* feel about your mate/spouse, taking into account the last few months. The rating you choose should reflect how you *actually* feel, not how you think you should feel or would like to feel.

> 1 = Extremely negative
> 2 = Quite negative
> 3 = Slightly negative
> 4 = Neutral
> 5 = Slightly positive
> 6 = Quite positive
> 7 = Extremely positive

_____ 1. How do you feel about your spouse as a friend to you?

_____ 2. How do you feel about the future of your marital relationship?

181

_____ 3. How do you feel about marrying/having married your spouse?

_____ 4. How do you feel about your spouse's ability to put you in a good mood so that you can laugh and smile?

_____ 5. How do you feel about your spouse's ability to handle stress?

_____ 6. How do you feel about the degree to which your spouse understands you?

_____ 7. How do you feel about the degree to which you can trust your spouse?

_____ 8. How do you feel about how your spouse relates to other people?

The following items are in the form of statements rather than questions. However, please complete them in the same manner, remembering to base your responses on how *you generally* feel about your spouse, taking into account the last few months.

1. Touching my spouse makes me feel _____
2. Being alone with my spouse makes me feel _____
3. Having sexual relations with my spouse makes me feel _____
4. Talking and communicating with my spouse makes me feel _____
5. My spouse's encouragement of my individual growth makes me feel _____
6. My spouse's physical appearance makes me feel ___
7. Seeking comfort from my spouse makes me feel ___

8.   Kissing my spouse makes me feel _____
9.   Sitting or lying close to my spouse makes me feel ___

SOURCE: K. Daniel O'Leary and Francis Fincham. "Assessment of Positive Feelings Toward Spouse." *Journal of Consulting and Clinical Psychology,* 1983, Vol. 51, pp. 949–951. Used by permission.

SCORING KEY

To find your score, simply add together the number you used for each item.

HOW DO YOU COMPARE?

SCORE		PERCENTILE
Men	*Women*	
88	94	15
94	99	30
101	104	50
107	109	70
113	114	85

About Positive Feelings

You undoubtedly already have a clear idea as to how you feel about your partner, but the *Positive Feelings Questionnaire* will give you a sense of how your feelings compare with other couples'. Dr. O'Leary and his colleagues at the State University of New York at Stonybrook developed this scale to measure changes in how men and women felt toward their spouses as they were going through marital therapy. The scale was successful in that the test scores of couples who were making progress in therapy tended to increase, but they also found that the scale was as effective at measuring general marital satisfaction as were other, established commercial tests. The norms provided here are for couples who were not in therapy. The scores for couples who were seeking marriage counseling were, as you might expect, considerably lower.

It is interesting to note differences between the scores of men and women on this test. Notice that the average score for women is slightly higher than the average score for men. But with couples who were seeking therapy, the average score for women was a full 10 points lower than the average score for men who were entering therapy. It seems that, in general, women might feel somewhat more positively toward their spouse than men, but with unhappily married couples, women have much more negative feelings than do their husbands. This is consistent with other studies that have found that women seeking a divorce have three times as many complaints as do their husbands.

Men and women do seem to have different reactions to long-term relationships. It has become almost a cliche to say that women are more concerned about relationships than men, but a cliche that contains a large grain of truth. I know that in my own experience in counseling couples, it is almost always the case that the woman initiated the therapy. At the beginning of the first session, when I ask what brought them in, the husband will invariably turn to his wife to invite her to outline her complaints. Typically, men spend more time defending themselves than complaining about their wives.

Women simply seem to think more about their relationships, and when things are not going the way they would like them to, they want to do something about it. Men, on the other hand, are likely to believe everything is fine as long as their partner isn't complaining too much. Many a time, a couple has come in during the course of therapy and the husband says something like, "We had a really good week. We didn't have a single argument." The wife then bursts into tears and responds, "That's because we hardly talked to each other." That men and women can have such different perceptions of their relationship can be both comic and tragic.

So what should you do if you would like to feel more positively toward your partner? Hundreds of books have been published that advise couples how to have happier and more satisfying relationships, and I would guess that most of these books offer good advice. But that so many authors have had so much to say about the subject certainly suggests that it is no easy matter to turn an unhappy marriage around. Even couples who spend the time, effort, and money to seek out professional counseling to save their relationship have less than a 50-50 chance of succeeding. Indeed, improving a bad relationship is very hard work.

This is a case where another cliche, "An ounce of prevention is worth a pound of cure," clearly applies. It is much easier to get into good habits early in the relationship, which will increase the odds that the relationship will be a happy one, than it is to turn things around once feelings of anger and resentment have taken hold. One good habit that every couple should strive to establish is to have regular and frequent pleasant interactions. Recent studies have found that couples who have five times as many pleasant interactions as unpleasant ones are likely to be happily married. If the percentage of unpleasant interactions rises much higher than twenty percent, the couple is likely to view the relationship as burdensome.

The pleasant interactions that are especially important are the simple, everyday kinds of things men and women can share. Telling your partner about an amusing article in the newspaper would count as a pleasant interaction; taking a walk around the block after dinner would count; sharing an experience from work would count; cuddling while watching a movie on TV would count. In other words, it is not necessary to plan exotic (and expensive) weekends away to have a solid relationship. It is necessary, however, to have five pleasant interactions to balance each heated discussion about the money running out before the end of the month, or problems with the children's discipline, or any other difficulty that is an inevitable part of every relationship. Too many couples only talk when they have a problem to discuss.

If your score was at the 50th percentile or higher, the odds are your relationship is in good condition; just keep on doing what you're doing. If you scored below the 50th percentile, you might want to attempt to increase your pleasant interactions. Don't be too ambitious. I've found that many couples try to completely remake their relationship and then give up when they find it too difficult. Start small. Tell your partner the joke you heard at work, tell your partner that he or she looks especially nice today, or reach across the table after dinner and give his or her hand a squeeze. Positive feelings almost always follow pleasant interactions.

SECTION V

GETTING IT ON

We have arrived at the nitty-gritty stuff now—your sexuality. After you complete this section, you will know—

A. How much you know about sex.
B. How your sexual attitudes compare with others'.
C. How anxious you are about your sexuality.
D. How sensual you are.
E. How satisfying your relationship is.

How Much Do You Know About Sex?

✓

THE SEXUAL KNOWLEDGE TEST

DIRECTIONS: For the following items, select the answer you think is correct.

_____ 1. The leading cause of birth defects in the United States is:
   a. cigarette smoking by mothers
   b. cocaine addiction by mothers
   c. alcohol abuse by mothers
   d. sexual activity during the later stages of pregnancy

_____ 2. Which of the following methods of birth control is probably the *least* safe for women?
   a. diaphragm
   b. condom
   c. IUD
   d. cervical cap

_____ 3. Women who feel guilty about sex are likely to:
  a. use contraceptives in an extremely effective fashion
  b. ignore their partner's preferences regarding contraception
  c. use contraceptives that require consultation with a physician
  d. make the least effective contraceptive decisions

_____ 4. Of the following, the contraceptive with the lowest failure rate, if used properly, is:
  a. the cervical cap
  b. the sponge
  c. withdrawal
  d. oral contraceptives

_____ 5. Over a period of one year, couples who have intercourse without using any form of contraception have a probability of pregnancy of about:
  a. 15 percent
  b. 40 percent
  c. 65 percent
  d. 90 percent

_____ 6. What fraction of boys and girls are likely to have had intercourse by age 19?
  a. one-third
  b. one-half
  c. two-thirds
  d. nine-tenths

_____ 7. About _____ percent of all Americans will marry by their late 30s.
  a. 75
  b. 85
  c. 90
  d. 95

_____ 8. In the 1990s, about _____ percent of American households were composed of single adults.

    a. 5

    b. 15

    c. 25

    d. 35

_____ 9. One important difference between the clitoris and the penis is that the clitoris:

    a. has relatively few nerve endings compared to the penis

    b. has no function other than sexual pleasure

    c. has no tissue that is equivalent to the foreskin of the penis

    d. cannot undergo erection

_____10. For women, hormones are directly involved in all of the following except:

    a. maintenance of pregnancy

    b. regulation of the menstrual cycle

    c. feelings of sexual desire

    d. ability to attain orgasm

_____11. When Mary has an orgasm, she notices that a clear liquid comes out of her vagina. Mary:

    a. may have vaginismus and should consult a physician

    b. may have a urinary tract infection and should consult a physician

    c. is experiencing normal vaginal sweating that occurs in all women during sexual excitement

    d. is experiencing a phenomenon that anywhere from 10 to 40 percent of women experience

_____12. The refractory period, the interval following an orgasm before a man can have another one, depends on:
   a. his feelings of attraction for his partner
   b. the intensity of his first orgasm
   c. his level of guilt regarding sexual matters
   d. his age

_____13. For most men:
   a. feelings of love diminish after many sexual encounters with a partner
   b. feelings of love and satisfaction with sexual encounters are almost completely independent
   c. feelings of love enhance the quality of sexual encounters
   d. sex without feelings of love is not especially enjoyable

_____14. Which of the following statements about masturbation is NOT true?
   a. men and women are about equally likely to masturbate
   b. masturbation occurs throughout the lifespan
   c. many people masturbate even when they have an available partner
   d. adolescent boys are more likely to talk about masturbation than adolescent girls

_____15. In which position do most women find it easiest to have an orgasm?
   a. man above
   b. woman above
   c. rear entry
   d. side-by-side

_____16. Various oral contraceptives work in slightly different ways, but they all:
   a. create a chemical state of "pregnancy" in the body
   b. form a barrier between egg and sperm
   c. prevent entry of the sperm into the uterus
   d. killing and weakening sperm

_____17. To maximize the chances of conceiving a child, intercourse should occur:
   a. six to ten days after the first day of the menstrual cycle
   b. four days before and one day after ovulation
   c. one to five days before menstruation
   d. three days before menstruation and two days after

_____18. The most common cause of infertility in women is:
   a. a history of substance abuse
   b. a history of previous abortion
   c. environmental toxins
   d. fallopian tube blockage

_____19. Which of the following is NOT a sign of menopause?
   a. hyperactivity
   b. hot flashes
   c. vaginal dryness
   d. insomnia

_____20. The most common sexual problem reported by men who seek therapy is:
   a. premature ejaculation
   b. erectile problems
   c. inability to ejaculate
   d. low sexual desire

_____21. Which of the following has NOT been found to cause erectile problems in men?
   a. arthritis
   b. lumbar-disc disease
   c. diabetes
   d. alcohol abuse

_____22. The type of therapy that has proved to be most effective in treating sexual problems of premature ejaculation, vaginismus, and women's inability to have orgasm is:
   a. cognitive-behavioral
   b. psychodynamic
   c. client-centered
   d. pharmacological

_____23. How many Americans are infected with a sexually transmitted disease every year?
   a. one to two million
   b. three to five million
   c. six to eight million
   d. twelve to thirteen million

_____24. The most common sexually transmitted disease in the United States is:
   a. chlamydia
   b. AIDS
   c. gonorrhea
   d. syphilis

_____25. Research has shown that people who read or watch sexually explicit material are likely to:
   a. have difficulty distinguishing between sexual fantasy and reality
   b. show a temporary increase in their typical sexual activities
   c. experiment with deviant or coercive sexual practices
   d. devalue their regular sexual partner

_____26. Modern researchers have concluded that the cause of homosexuality in men is:
   a. related to pathological experiences during childhood
   b. genetic background
   c. hormonal problems during fetal development
   d. unknown for certain at this time

_____27. Production of testosterone in men:
   a. declines gradually beginning around age 40
   b. declines suddenly during the man's middle 50s
   c. remains relatively constant throughout the lifespan
   d. varies so much from man to man that no generalizations can be made

_____28. With regard to the observation that men seem to have a greater interest in sex than women, experts:
   a. agree that such a difference does not exist in reality; men are simply more willing to admit to sexual interest
   b. agree that the difference results from social forces; while boys are encouraged to show interest in sex, girls are discouraged from doing so
   c. agree that this difference has a biological basis
   d. disagree as to whether it results from biology or from social forces

_____29. As males move through middle age:
   a. the urgency of their sex drive decreases
   b. they require more physical stimulation to achieve an erection
   c. they must wait longer after having an orgasm before they can have another
   d. all of the above

_____30. The best predictor of how a woman will respond sexually after menopause is:
   a. the degree of reduction in her estrogen level
   b. the severity of the symptoms experienced during menopause
   c. her attitude toward sex
   d. the attitude of her partner toward her menopause

_____31. A man who becomes especially excited when his partner wears her old cheerleader outfit when they make love:
   a. suffers from a psychiatric disorder
   b. has the potential to abuse children
   c. enjoys humiliating his sexual partners
   d. is within the normal range of sexual behavior

_____32. Studies of bisexuality have established that:
   a. true bisexuality is virtually nonexistent
   b. for at least some people, sexual orientation may not be as stable as we tend to assume
   c. most people who call themselves bisexual are in fact homosexual, but have difficulty in acknowledging this
   d. bisexuals are twice as likely to get a date come Saturday night

SOURCE: Louis H. Janda, "The Sexual Knowledge Test." Unpublished manuscript, 1994. Old Dominion University.

SCORING KEY

Give yourself one point for each correct answer which can be found on the following page.

1. c	12. d	23. d
2. c	13. c	24. a
3. d	14. a	25. b
4. d	15. b	26. d
5. d	16. a	27. a
6. c	17. b	28. d
7. c	18. d	29. d
8. c	19. a	30. c
9. b	20. d	31. d
10. d	21. a	32. b
11. d	22. a	

HOW DO YOU COMPARE?

SCORE	PERCENTILE
13	15
16	30
19	50
22	70
25	85

About Sexual Knowledge

Sex is a natural part of life. There is no need to try to learn about it. When the time comes, you'll know what to do. Right?

If you are educated and inquisitive enough to read this book, I'm sure you will not agree with the above statement, but it surprises me how many people do believe that it is pointless to become well informed about sex. Eating is a natural part of life as well, but it is obvious to most everyone that we can have healthier, more satisfying, and longer lives if we are well informed about food. The same is true when it comes to sex. Being well informed can certainly increase our health and our satisfaction, and in this day of AIDS, knowledge can mean life itself.

Let me say a few words about this particular test. There are a few similar tests published by other sex educators, but one researcher failed to give me permission to use his, and the other tests I looked at had too many questions about matters that I considered inconsequential. So I made my own test. I started with a large pool of items that I believe reflected information that most people would find useful in their everyday lives, and I used the students in my Psychology of Sex course at Old Dominion University to generate the statistics necessary to construct a test. I won't bore you with the details, but this test is both reliable and valid. The students' scores on this test were strongly related to their final grades in my course. Because the norms are based on college students who had nearly completed a course in human sexuality, your score may pale by comparison. But if you did score at the 50th percentile or higher, you should congratulate yourself. You are very well informed about sex.

One reason it is important to be knowledgeable about sex is because our sexual behavior is so closely tied in with our psychology. Our beliefs and attitudes can influence both our behavior and our body's reaction. The renowned sex researchers Masters and Johnson gave a classic example of this nearly twenty-five years ago. They found that a common cause of erectile problems in men was a failure experience associated with alcohol. Masters and Johnson described a composite case in which a middle-aged man had more to drink than usual one evening and then decided he was in the mood for love. Much to his dismay, nothing happened, but he attributed his failure to his advancing years rather than the alcohol. The man worried that his failure was a signal that he was getting too old for that sort of thing, and this fear made it impossible to respond during subsequent encounters. Had this man been knowledgeable about sex, he would have simply said to himself something such as, "Well, I overdid the booze tonight, but wait until tomorrow. I'll be raring to go." There are countless other examples that sex therapists have written about in which ignorance caused a problem where none existed.

A second reason to be well informed is that knowledge does seem to lead to more responsible behavior. This point goes to the heart of the controversy over sex education in the public schools, but there is evidence that well-designed, school-based sex education programs do lead to lower rates of teenage pregnancy and sexually transmitted diseases. And contrary to the fears of parents who oppose sex education, such programs do not lead to experimentation at earlier ages or promiscuity.

My goal for this test was to prepare items that reflected facts. But the truth is that for many issues, not all experts agree on what the facts are. It was only a century ago that physicians were busy naming diseases that could result from excessive masturbation. And the first wave of "Marriage Manuals" published during the early part of this century warned men not to impose themselves on their wives too often because it could cause their wives physical harm. It is wise to be skeptical when any expert (except me, of course) tries to tell you the "facts."

In this spirit, let me briefly discuss a few items for which other experts might take issue with the alternative I selected as correct. Item 11 asks about Mary, who notices that a clear liquid comes out of her vagina when she has an orgasm. You may know that some experts have claimed that women ejaculate during orgasm. They claim to have identified anatomical structures that are associated with female ejaculation, known as the G-spot, and to have demonstrated that the female ejaculate is not simply urine. Other researchers report that they cannot find a G-spot and that the female ejaculate is, in fact, urine. While I'm skeptical about the reality of female ejaculation, it is clearly the case that many women experience a phenomenon similar to the one Mary does, and it should not be considered abnormal.

Item 20 reflects a lively debate among experts as to why low sexual desire has become so common among men. Interestingly, according to some social scientists, it may be the sex experts themselves who have led to the large number of men who seek therapy for low sexual desire. When Masters and Johnson published their book *Human Sexual Inadequacy* in 1970, premature ejaculation was reported to be the most common sexual problem among men. But as experts and the popular writers they inspired began to convey the message that it was possible for everyone to experience sexual ecstasy with the right training, many people began to feel inadequate. Thirty years ago, a 50-year-old man whose sexual interest was waning may have simply thought that was the way things were supposed to be, and both he and his wife would accept that. Today, when women's magazines are filled with articles about increasing one's sexual vitality, it should not be surprising that so many middle-aged men are concluding that they must have a problem if they do not experience the same level of sexual interest that they did when they were 20.

Item 26 asks about the cause of homosexuality in men. When I first began teaching Psychology of Sex in the late 1970s, I told my students that there was no evidence that homosexuality was biological, and that most experts agreed that it resulted from experiences during childhood. Well, things have changed since then, and now I tell my students about several intriguing studies that do suggest a biological basis for homosexuality. But the fact remains that we simply do not have conclusive answers to this question. I personally believe that both experiences and biology contribute to a homosexual orientation, but I could be proved wrong by research conducted over the next 20 years. We just don't know for sure. Any expert who claims to have the final answer is either not much of an expert or is being disingenuous.

The issue of homosexuality is interesting, because it demonstrates that "facts" about sex can change. Sometimes experts are just plain wrong, as they were when they claimed that masturbation could lead to various diseases. Other times experts may provide the best answer, as I did with my students fifteen years ago, given the status of the evidence. But as research techniques become more sophisticated, the evidence can change, as it has with regard to homosexuality. The moral of the story is that it is especially crucial to be well informed about human sexuality so that you can evaluate the latest claims made by the experts. We're not always right.

What Do You Think About Sex?

✓

THE SEXUAL ATTITUDES SCALE

DIRECTIONS: Several statements that reflect different attitudes about sex are listed below. For each statement, fill in the response that indicates how much you agree or disagree with that statement. Some of the items refer to a specific sexual relationship, whereas others refer to general attitudes and beliefs about sex. Whenever possible, answer the questions with your current partner in mind. If you are not currently in a relationship, answer the questions with your most recent partner in mind. If you have never had a sexual relationship, answer in terms of what you think your responses would most likely be.

For each statement:
    1 = strongly disagree with the statement
    2 = moderately disagree with the statement
    3 = neutral—neither agree nor disagree
    4 = moderately agree with the statement
    5 = strongly agree with the statement

_____ 1. I do not need to be committed to a person to have sex with him or her.

_____ 2. Casual sex is acceptable.

_____ 3. I would like to have sex with many partners.

_____ 4. One-night stands are sometimes very enjoyable.

_____ 5. It is OK to have ongoing sexual relationships with more than one person at a time.

_____ 6. It is OK to manipulate someone into having sex as long as no future promises are made.

_____ 7. Sex as a simple exchange of favors is OK if both people agree to it.

_____ 8. The best sex is with no strings attached.

_____ 9. Life would have fewer problems if people could have sex more freely.

_____10. It is possible to enjoy sex with a person and not like that person very much.

_____11. Sex is more fun with someone you don't love.

_____12. It is all right to pressure someone into having sex.

_____13. Extensive premarital sexual experience is fine.

_____14. Extramarital affairs are all right as long as one's partner doesn't know about them.

_____15. Sex for its own sake is perfectly all right.

_____16. I would feel comfortable having intercourse with my partner in the presence of other people.

_____17. Prostitution is acceptable.

_____18. It is OK for sex to be just good physical release.

_____19. Sex without love is meaningless.

_____20. People should at least be friends before they have sex together.

_____21. In order for sex to be good, it must also be meaningful.

_____22. Birth control is part of responsible sexuality.

_____23. A woman should share responsibility for birth control.

_____24. A man should share responsibility for birth control.

_____25. Sex education is important for young people.

_____26. Using "sex toys" during lovemaking is acceptable.

_____27. Masturbation is all right.

_____28. Masturbating one's partner during intercourse can increase the pleasure of sex.

_____29. Sex gets better as a relationship progresses.

_____30. Sex is the closest form of communication between two people.

_____31. A sexual encounter between two people deeply in love is the ultimate human interaction.

_____32. Orgasm is the greatest experience in the world.

_____33. At its best, sex seems to be the merging of two souls.

_____34. Sex is a very important part of life.

_____35. Sex is usually an intensive, almost overwhelming experience.

_____36. During sexual intercourse, intense awareness of the partner is the best frame of mind.

_____37. Sex is fundamentally good.

_____ 38. Sex is best when you let yourself go and focus on your own pleasure.

_____ 39. Sex is primarily the taking of pleasure from another person.

_____ 40. The main purpose of sex is to enjoy oneself.

_____ 41. Sex is primarily physical.

_____ 42. Sex is primarily a bodily function, like eating.

_____ 43. Sex is mostly a game between males and females.

SOURCE: Susan Hendrick and Clyde Hendrick. "Multidimensionality of Sexual Attitudes." *The Journal of Sex Research,* 1987, 502–526. Used by permission.

SCORING KEY FOR THE
SEXUAL ATTITUDES INVENTORY

From their research, the Hendricks concluded that there are four primary dimensions of sexual attitudes, so for this scale you will be calculating scores for four subscales. For each of the subscales, add together your score for each item. The first dimension is *Permissiveness* which includes items 1–21 (items 19, 20, and 21 are reverse scored, which means that you should subtract your number from 6). Items 22–28 comprise the *Sexual Practices* scale, items 29–37 are on the *Communion* scale, and items 38–43 define the *Instrumentality* scale. The norms, as is the case with almost all the scales, are based on college students, who tend to be somewhat more liberal in their sexual attitudes than the general population.

HOW DO YOU COMPARE?

	SCORE Men	Women	PERCENTILE
Permissiveness	34	21	15
	47	25	30
	60	38	50
	73	51	70
	86	64	85
Sexual Practices	18	18	15
	22	22	30
	28	28	50
	32	32	70
	35	35	85
Communion	26	26	15
	31	31	30
	36	36	50
	41	41	70
	45	45	85
Instrumentality	9	6	15
	13	10	30
	17	14	50
	21	18	70
	24	22	85

About Sexual Attitudes

There are hundreds of measures of sexual attitudes that focus on dozens of different dimensions, but husband-and-wife psychologists Clyde and Susan Hendrick believed that it would be helpful to researchers in the field of human sexuality to have a single, wide-ranging scale that could be used to measure several components of sexual attitudes at one time. To this end they constructed their Sexual Attitudes Scale. Using a statistical technique called factor analysis, they concluded that sexual attitudes are made up of four primary components, which they called Permissiveness, Sexual Practices, Communion, and Instrumentality.

The Permissiveness dimension is self-explanatory. The higher your score, the more permissive and liberal your sexual attitudes are. Compared to low scorers, people with high scores are likely to have had more sexual relationships, to have engaged in a greater variety of sexual practices, and to believe that love isn't a necessary prerequisite for sex. These people have a lot in common with the "Sensation-Seekers" described in Section II. They are likely to become easily bored and are constantly on the lookout for new experiences—sexual and otherwise. Interestingly, although their relationships are relatively weak, people high in sexual permissiveness tend to have somewhat higher self-esteem than sexually conservative people.

The Sexual Practices dimension reflects what the Hendricks call responsible, tolerant sexuality. People who score high on this component tend to be accepting of their sexuality and value this aspect of their lives, and they place much importance on behaving in a sexually responsible manner. These people are similar to highly permissive people in that they value new sexual experiences, but unlike them they believe that it is important to conform to society's norms when engaging in novel behavior. Another important difference between Sexual Practices and Permissiveness is that the high scorers in the former tend to have more intimate verbal interactions with their partners. These people place a high value on communication between sexual partners.

People who score high in the Communion subscale tend to have a very emotional, idealistic approach to sex. As the items in this dimension suggest, people whose highest score is in this scale tend to believe that the spiritual elements of sexual intercourse are more important than the physical act. They value the pleasure they receive in their relationship, but they view this pleasure as a means of bringing them closer to their partner, as a means of strengthening the bond between the two of them. These people find it difficult to even imagine having sex with someone they do not care about deeply. Your score on this subscale depends in part on your current relationship status. In their surveys, the Hendricks found that those people who answered yes to the question "Are you in love now?" were more likely to score high on Communion than those who responded in the negative. Interestingly, people who said that they had been in love "several times" were high on Permissiveness compared to those who had more limited experience. It seems that being in love makes one idealistic about sex, but this idealism may be eroded by too many such experiences.

Finally, the Instrumentality dimension reflects a somewhat selfish, egocentric view of sexual relationships. High scorers tend to be "game-players." They believe it is okay to deceive and manipulate potential partners if it gets them what they want. These people have much in common with highly permissive people, but they tend to be more cynical in their approach to sexual relationships. It should come as a surprise to no one that these individuals have little interest in developing emotionally intimate relationships with their sexual partners.

As you can see from the norms, men and women tend to have different attitudes toward sex; men are higher in Permissiveness and Instrumentality. As all good psychologists must do when they publish in scientific journals, the Hendricks discussed these differences using technical jargon, but I don't think it is oversimplifying to say that their research tended to be consistent with the old cliche "Men give love to get sex while women give sex to get love."

As is always the case, you and your partner will be most satisfied if your scores in the four dimensions are similar. In most relationships, the man is likely to be higher in Permissiveness and Instrumentality, so you should not be concerned if your partner's scores are somewhat different from your own. On the other hand, if your highest score is in Communion and your partner's is in Instrumentality, you both have a lot of talking to do if you are going to make your relationship work.

How Anxious Are You About Your Sexuality?

✓

THE SEXUAL ANXIETY INVENTORY

DIRECTIONS: Each of the sentence stems below is followed by two alternatives that complete it. Your task is to pick the one that better describes your feelings. It may be the case that neither alternative describes your feelings exactly. If this is true, pick the one that comes closer to describing how you feel.

_____ 1. Extramarital sex
   a. is OK if everyone agrees.
   b. can break up families.

_____ 2. Sex
   a. can cause as much anxiety as pleasure.
   b. on the whole is good and enjoyable.

_____ 3. Masturbation
   a. causes me to worry.
   b. can be a useful substitute.

_____ 4. After having sexual thoughts
   a. I feel aroused.
   b. I feel jittery.

_____ 5. When I engage in petting
   a. I feel scared at first.
   b. I thoroughly enjoy it.

_____ 6. Initiating sexual relationships
   a. is a very stressful experience.
   b. causes me no problem at all.

_____ 7. Oral sex
   a. would arouse me.
   b. would terrify me.

_____ 8. I feel nervous
   a. about initiating sexual relations.
   b. about nothing when it comes to members of the opposite sex.

_____ 9. When I meet someone I'm attracted to
   a. I get to know him or her.
   b. I feel nervous.

_____ 10. When I was younger
   a. I was looking forward to having sex.
   b. I felt nervous about the prospect of having sex.

_____ 11. When others flirt with me
   a. I don't know what to do.
   b. I flirt back.

_____ 12. Group sex
   a. would scare me to death.
   b. might be interesting.

_____ 13. If in the future I committed adultery
   a. I would probably get caught.
   b. I wouldn't feel bad about it.

_____14. I would
    a. feel too nervous to tell a dirty joke in mixed company.
    b. tell a dirty joke if it was funny.

_____15. Dirty jokes
    a. make me feel uncomfortable.
    b. often make me laugh.

_____16. When I awake from sexual dreams
    a. I feel pleasant and relaxed.
    b. I feel tense.

_____17. When I have sexual desires
    a. I worry about what I should do.
    b. I do something to satisfy them.

_____18. If in the future I committed adultery
    a. it would be nobody's business but my own.
    b. I would worry about my spouse's finding out.

_____19. Buying a pornographic book
    a. wouldn't bother me.
    b. would make me nervous.

_____20. Casual sex
    a. is better than no sex at all.
    b. can hurt many people.

_____21. Extramarital sex
    a. is sometimes necessary.
    b. can damage one's career.

_____22. Sexual advances
    a. leave me feeling tense.
    b. are welcomed.

_____23. When I have sexual relations
   a. I feel satisfied.
   b. I worry about being discovered.

_____24. When talking about sex in mixed company
   a. I feel nervous.
   b. I sometimes get excited.

_____25. If I were to flirt with someone
   a. I would worry about his or her reaction.
   b. I would enjoy it.

SOURCE: Louis H. Janda and Kevin E. O'Grady. "Development of a Sex Anxiety Inventory." *Journal of Consulting and Clinical Psychology,* 1980, *48,* 169–175.

SCORING KEY FOR THE
SEXUAL ANXIETY INVENTORY

1.	b	14.	a
2.	a	15.	a
3.	a	16.	b
4.	b	17.	a
5.	a	18.	b
6.	a	19.	b
7.	b	20.	b
8.	a	21.	b
9.	b	22.	a
10.	b	23.	b
11.	a	24.	a
12.	a	25.	a
13.	a		

HOW DO YOU COMPARE?

Score		Percentile
Men	Women	
2	6	15
5	9	30
8	12	50
11	15	70
14	18	85

About Sexual Anxiety

I was interested in developing this scale to measure sex anxiety, along with my graduate student, Kevin O'Grady, in order to learn more about possible distinctions between guilt and anxiety. Psychologist Donald Mosher had constructed a measure of sex guilt that had been used extensively in research and before I say more about sex anxiety, let me tell you a little about guilt. Sex guilt can be thought of as a tendency to refrain from sexual behavior because one anticipates feeling bad about himself or herself for violating his or her standards of proper behavior. As you might expect, people who are high in guilt have fewer sexual experiences than do people who are low in this dimension. But even guilty people have sex, and contrary to what you might expect, their guilt seems to make it difficult for them to be responsible in their sexual relationships. For instance, young women who are high in guilt wait much longer than women low in guilt before starting to use contraceptives. Guilty young men find it so difficult to walk into a drugstore to buy a box of condoms that they would rather take a chance on getting their partner pregnant or contracting a sexually transmitted disease. Guilt is rarely powerful enough to keep people from expressing their sexuality, but it does seem to make it difficult for them to talk about it openly with their partner. And if partners do not communicate about their relationship, the chances are they will engage in risky behavior.

Kevin O'Grady and I noticed that there are lots of people who do not think that sexuality is shameful or immoral, but nonetheless, they seem to have very restricted sex lives. Perhaps, we reasoned, they're not guilty about sex, but they may have a lot of anxiety associated with sexual issues. The difference between guilt and anxiety can be seen in the very first item on this scale dealing with extramarital sex. Mosher's guilt scale has a similar item, but guilty people say they would avoid an affair because it would be wrong or they would feel bad about themselves. What these people think of themselves is far more important to them than how others view them. Anxious people would also avoid having an affair, but because they are worried about what might happen to them. Anxious people are not troubled by thoughts of right or wrong, but they are likely to worry about getting caught by their spouse or losing their job. So guilty people and anxious people may behave in very similar ways but for very different reasons.

One additional note about the relation between guilt and anxiety: they tend to go together. While there are some people who have very little sex guilt and a high level of sex anxiety (the converse is also true), most people who are guilty about sex tend to be anxious about it as well. What about you? How does your sex anxiety compare with your sex guilt?

One important and very practical implication of both guilt and anxiety is that people with lots of both are more likely than others to develop sexual dysfunctions. A thorough discussion of this issue could fill an entire book, but here is one important difference between people who score high and those who score low on this scale: they tend to understand their bodily responses to sexual stimulation in different ways. Let me give you an example. Suppose a man, who tends to be quite anxious when it comes to sex, has been dating a woman for a while and the magic moment has arrived—they are in his bedroom for the first time and she is slowly unbuttoning his shirt. Our subject notices that his heart is pounding wildly, and his palms are so moist that he is surreptitiously drying them on the bedspread so as not to stain his partner's blouse when it comes time for him to do the honors. He can't help but notice these reactions and he says to himself, "My god, I'm scared to death. This is going to be a disaster. I'll never get it up." Our second subject, who is low in guilt and anxiety, finds himself in the same situation and has the same bodily reactions. Only he says to himself, "My god, I haven't been this excited in ages. This is going to be really great!" There is a good chance both of these men are creating self-fulfilling prophecies, and what the first man is telling himself may lead to a sexual dysfunction.

If you had a low score on the Sex Anxiety Inventory, it is likely that you have the ability to rejoice in your sexuality and act responsibly about it. If your score placed you above the 85th percentile, it does not mean you are pathological, since this scale was constructed for normal adults. But you would be wise to make sure that you do not create your own negative self-fulfilling prophecies. And most important, do not allow your nervousness to keep you from communicating with your partner about birth control and safe sex.

How Sensual Are You?

THE SENSUALITY SCALE

DIRECTIONS: For the following items, if the statement generally describes you, respond with a "T." If it does not generally describe you, respond with an "F."

_____ 1. When talking with friends, I like to stand close to them.

_____ 2. Overall, my body is fairly sensitive.

_____ 3. I usually notice how the fabric of my clothing feels against my body.

_____ 4. I would enjoy taking a sauna.

_____ 5. One can never get enough of a good thing.

_____ 6. I think people should display affection more openly.

_____ 7. I enjoy the feeling when a cat rubs up against me.

_____ 8. I believe people should live for the pleasure of the moment.

_____ 9. When dancing, I prefer to hold my partner close.

_____10. When looking at a work of art, I examine it carefully.

_____ 11. I enjoy petting dogs and cats.

_____12. I like to taste exotic and unusual foods.

_____13. When looking at a painting, I try to absorb its essence and deeper meaning.

_____14. I like it when friends touch me while talking to me.

_____15. My sense of smell is somewhat better than average.

_____16. I sometimes feel things more deeply than others.

_____17. God did not put people on earth so they could have fun.

_____18. I prefer dancing to slow, romantic music.

_____19. Many foods taste the same to me.

_____20. As far as flowers are concerned, if you've seen one, you've seen them all.

_____21. I seldom wear perfume or cologne.

_____22. When reading a good story, I sometimes have deep feelings about it.

_____23. In planning a meal, I can almost taste the food by just thinking about it.

_____24. I like the feeling of a soft breeze against my skin.

_____25. I enjoy sunbathing.

_____26. Too much pleasure is sinful.

_____27. I enjoy taking a long, hot bath.

_____28. When I'm alone, I like to wear as little as possible.

_____29. I sometimes like to sleep in the nude.

_____30. I like the smell of incense and scented candles.

_____31. I like curving, flowing lines better than straight lines with sharp angles.

_____32. I am excited by the sound of a large orchestra.

_____33. I enjoy the smell of freshly cut grass.

_____34. I like to wear soft fabrics, such as nylon or silk.

_____35. I like foods that are succulent and juicy.

_____36. I think skinny-dipping would be enjoyable.

_____37. I seldom notice the smell of flowers.

SOURCE: Jerry Fulk. "The Development of a Scale to Measure Sensuality." Honors Thesis, 1994. Old Dominion University. Used by permission.

SCORING KEY

1. T	13. T	25. T
2. T	14. T	26. F
3. T	15. T	27. T
4. T	16. T	28. T
5. T	17. F	29. T
6. T	18. T	30. T
7. T	19. F	31. T
8. T	20. F	32. T
9. T	21. F	33. T
10. T	22. T	34. T
11. T	23. T	35. T
12. T	24. T	36. T
		37. F

HOW DO YOU COMPARE?

Score		Percentile
Men	Women	
17	21	15
20	24	30
23	27	50
26	30	70
29	33	85

About Sensuality

One of the real pleasures of being a college professor is working with students who challenge you in such a way that you end up seeing things from a different perspective. Jerry Fulk, who constructed this Sensuality Scale, is one of those students. He was in my Psychology of Sex class, and at the end of the semester he asked if he could do a research project under my supervision. I readily agreed, since he was one of the best students in the course, but when I heard his idea for a project I wondered if I hadn't spoken too soon. His review of the professional journals turned up a number of scales measuring a variety of aspects of human sexuality, but he could not find one to measure a characteristic that he was interested in—sensuality. That sounded well and good, but when he told me about some of the items he thought would tap this dimension, I was sure his project would be a waste of time. After all, what could curvy lines, paintings, or freshly cut grass possibly have to do with sensuality? But, being the open-minded person I am, I told him to go ahead; I would help him with his project. At the very least, I thought, he would learn something about the difficulties of constructing personality tests.

Jerry worked hard. He generated an original pool of some 80 items, administered this preliminary form of the test to more than 100 people, and generated the appropriate statistics.

When I saw the results, I couldn't believe it. The statistics convincingly demonstrated that most of his items about curvy lines, looking at paintings, petting dogs, and the like were indeed measuring something important. Items such as "I can be sexually aroused quite easily," which I insisted he include because they seemed more directly related to sensuality, turned out not to be very useful and hence did not make it to this final version of the scale.

Our research did find that this scale was able to predict several elements of sexual behavior. Scores on this scale, for instance, are related to the age at which one has sex for the first time, the frequency with which one has sex, how long one's average sexual encounter lasts, and how much one enjoys simple touching and caressing. Nothing surprising about any of that. But especially fascinating was the finding that scores on this scale are not related to frequency of sexual fantasies, frequency of masturbation, overall importance of sex, or overall importance of having an orgasm.

In retrospect, it all makes sense. When it comes to sensuality and sex, there are two kinds of people in this world. At the low end of the continuum are those who may have strong sexual urges, but who are not all that interested in savoring their sexual encounters. For such men and women, sex is primarily a matter of releasing their pent-up sexual energy, so it is not surprising that their sexual encounters are relatively brief. People who are high in sensuality are more interested in the process of sex than in the end result. These people enjoy the simple pleasures of touching and caressing perhaps as much as the more intense pleasures of orgasm. They want their sexual encounters to go on as long as possible.

The items on the scale also suggest that this trait of sensuality is not specific to sex, but cuts across all five of our senses and influences our reactions in a variety of situations. Sensual people enjoy tactile stimulation of all kinds; they like their friends to touch them while conversing, they like petting cats and dogs, and they like the feel of silk against their skin. These people are sensual when eating. They enjoy unusual, exotic, and succulent foods. They take pleasure in their sense of smell; they enjoy the smell of freshly cut grass, and they like to wear perfumes and colognes. The items about looking at works of art suggest that these people can gratify their need for sensual experiences through their eyes. And even the sense of hearing plays a part, as suggested by the item "I am excited by the sound of a large orchestra."

These items suggest a practical use. One may want to evaluate potential lovers by taking them to an unusual restaurant, a petting zoo, an art gallery, or the symphony. Their reactions may very well say something about what they will be like in more intimate settings.

While people low in sensuality may seem like a joyless, ascetic lot, sensuality can cause problems for some people. Sensual people are somewhat hedonistic. They enjoy the pleasures that life can afford and believe that one can never get too much of a good thing. This tendency may lead to irresponsible sexual behavior and a greater likelihood of abusing mood-altering substances. One can certainly overdo a good thing.

No one, I'm sure, will be surprised by the finding that on average, women have higher scores on the Sensuality Scale than do men. Every expert who has ever offered advice has pointed out that women tend to like the romance that precedes a sexual encounter and lots of foreplay before intercourse is initiated. While some men are highly sensual, in general they tend to be the "let's get to it" type. On the whole, they simply aren't as interested in the preliminaries. Despite the hundreds of books and articles that have offered advice on how to deal with this dilemma, I doubt that an ideal solution exists. Perhaps the best that couples can do is compromise. Men should make a genuine effort to satisfy all their partner's sensual needs on at least some of their encounters. And women would be well advised, at least on occasion, to gratify their partner's desire for quick and furious sex.

How Satisfying Is Your Relationship?

✓

> ## THE RELATIONSHIP ASSESSMENT SCALE

DIRECTIONS: Please mark the letter for each item that best answers that item for you:

1. How well does your partner meet your needs?

A	B	C	D	E
Poorly		Average		Extremely Well

2. In general, how satisfied are you with your relationship?

A	B	C	D	E
Unsatisfied		Average		Extremely Satisfied

3. How good is your relationship compared to most?

A	B	C	D	E
Poor		Average		Excellent

4. How often do you wish you hadn't gotten in this relationship?

A	B	C	D	E
Never		Average		Very Often

5. To what extent has your relationship met your original expectations?

    A   B   C   D   E
    Hardly at all   Average   Completely

6. How much do you love your partner?

    A   B   C   D   E
    Not much   Average   Very much

7. How many problems are there in your relationship?

    A   B   C   D   E
    Very few   Average   Very many

SOURCE: Susan S. Hendrick. "A generic Measure of relationship satisfaction." *Journal of Marriage and the Family,* 1988, Vol. 50, 93–98. Used by permission.

SCORING KEY FOR THE
RELATIONSHIP ASSESSMENT SCALE

To find your score, use the key below:

A = 1 point
B = 2 points
C = 3 points
D = 4 points
E = 5 points

Items 4 and 7 are reverse scored, so for these two items subtract your score from 6 before finding your total by adding your points for all seven items.

HOW DO YOU COMPARE?

Score	Percentile
23	15
26	30
29	50
32	70
35	85

About Relationship Satisfaction

Don't be fooled by the brevity of this scale. Constructed by Dr. Susan Hendrick of Texas Tech University, it is both valid and efficient. Dr. Hendrick found that it correlated highly with a widely used, commercially published inventory of marital satisfaction. And her scale did better than the commercial inventory at predicting which dating college couples would be together a semester later. Good things can be found in small packages—even in psychology.

If you've been in your relationship for some time, you might find the norms a bit unnerving. Dr. Hendricks used college students who reported they were "in love" as the standardization group. Since a majority of these couples were in relationships of relatively brief duration, they were probably still viewing their partner through the rose-colored glasses of romantic love. These norms will give you a good basis for comparison if you are in a relatively new relationship, but if you've been with your partner for a number of years, take them with a large grain of salt. You might find it more instructive to compare your responses with your partner's. Dr. Hendrick reported that couples who stayed together (for at least a semester) tended to have quite similar ratings.

Why an inventory for relationship satisfaction in the section dealing with sexuality? The answer is probably obvious, but there is a clear link between relationship satisfaction and sexual satisfaction. Various studies have reported slightly different results, but all researchers agree that both men and women who are happy with their relationship and feel emotionally close to their partner are more likely to experience sexual satisfaction. Men who consider themselves happily married are much more likely than their unhappy counterparts to rate their sexual encounters as highly pleasurable. And women who are happily married are much more likely than unhappily married women to have orgasm regularly. There are, however, a substantial number of men and a sizable minority of women who do thoroughly enjoy their sexual encounters even though they are dissatisfied with their overall relationship.

It might surprise you to learn that there is not a particularly strong correspondence between frequency of sex and marital satisfaction. In one interesting study, the researchers examined the link between number of arguments and frequency of intercourse with marital satisfaction. Contrary to what you might expect, neither the number of arguments nor the frequency of sex was related to satisfaction with the relationship, but the frequency of sex minus the number of arguments did predict marital satisfaction. The moral of the story is obvious. If you have a serious argument with your spouse, be sure to make love several times before you let that happen again.

This link between relationship satisfaction and sexual satisfaction does have important implications, should you find your sex life wanting. There have been dozens, perhaps hundreds, of books written advising couples how they can revitalize their sex lives, and a majority of these books focus on sexual techniques. Much of this advice emphasizes the importance of novelty; couples are advised to try new activities in new settings. They may be told to rent sexy movies or to discuss their fantasies with each other. Women may be encouraged to take the initiative, to do something out of character—such as greeting their husband dressed in nothing but cellophane wrap. These techniques can work for some couples, at least in the short run. But eventually, even the novel becomes routine.

A more enduring solution may be to work on improving the overall quality of the relationship. There is evidence to suggest that women who discuss their feelings with their partner are more likely to experience sexual satisfaction. And as men grow older, they are likely to report that their desire to have sex is more closely tied to their wanting to express their love and affection than to satisfy their physical lust.

Couples who want to improve their sex lives may be well advised to spend more time talking with each other. They might try to find activities (other than sex) that they can enjoy together. They could make a conscious effort to verbalize their feelings of love, respect, and admiration for each other. If they can feel good about their relationship and see themselves as lucky to have their partner, they are likely to find their sexual encounters pleasurable as well.

As urgent and compelling as sexual desire can seem when one is 20 years old and looking for a partner, it is actually rather fragile. Sex therapists have reported that inhibited sexual desire has become the most common problem for both men and women who are seeking therapy. There are never any easy answers, but if a couple's sex life has become humdrum, it will be almost impossible for it to improve unless they can feel good about their overall relationship.

Epilogue

As I said at the beginning of this book, I hope you learned something useful about yourself by taking these tests. Since they are "self-report" inventories, the chances are you had a pretty good idea of how you would score before you even completed the various tests, but it can be helpful to have some idea of how you stand relative to others.

I suspect the most valuable aspect of going through this book is that it might help you focus your thoughts. For instance, you may have realized that you felt uncomfortable when trying for that promotion, but were never able to articulate to yourself exactly what was going on. Perhaps the Impostor Phenomenon Scale or the Fear of Success Scale gave you some insight into your situation and hence some idea how you might get past this obstacle. Or perhaps the Interpersonal Dependency Scale helped you to better understand some of the conflicts you have been having with your partner.

A second benefit of taking these tests is that you probably never thought about a few of the traits that were covered. The Internality, Chance, and Powerful Others Scale and the Sensation-Seeking Scale, to name two tests, measure characteristics that can have an important effect on our lives, but they are not traits that are widely discussed outside of academic psychology. I hope you were able to learn a few things about yourself that you hadn't known before.

Finally, if you haven't already, I urge you to go through

these tests with that important person in your life. I hate
to sound like such a typical psychologist, but it is true that
the better you understand someone, the more likely your
relationship will be successful. Since most of us see ourselves in ways that can be much different from how others
see us, you might come to understand your partner better
if you complete the scales as you think your partner
would, and then compare your responses with your partner's.

Let me repeat something I said in the introduction because it is so important. Almost without exception, the
scales in this book were constructed to be used in research
with normal populations. So, you may not be thrilled with
some of the scores you received, but the information in
this book provides absolutely no basis for you to conclude
that you have any serious psychological problems. Yes, it
may point to areas in your life that you would like to
change, but there is nothing in here that should cause you
to despair. I wouldn't do that to you.

I hope you enjoyed taking these tests as much as I enjoyed putting them together for you. Good luck with any
changes you try to make, and have a happy and satisfying
life.